401K Tune-up

401K Tune-up

Do you really want to work 'til 80?

Hugh W. Connelly, CFA, CFS

Library of Congress Control Number:		2012923842
ISBN:	Hardcover	978-1-4797-6891-2
	Softcover	978-1-4797-6890-5
	Ebook	978-1-4797-6892-9

To order additional copies of this book, contact:
Xlibris Corporation
1-888-795-4274
www.Xlibris.com
Orders@Xlibris.com
109198

Contents

Dedication

It has been said that "behind every great man, is a great woman." Today's interpretation of this axiom is "beside every great man is a great woman." In my life, there has been one great person by my side since 1986 when we first met, my wife, Diane. Diane or "Dee" as she is known by the family has been an amazing partner for me. Every time I have a "great idea" she listens and offers support, not ridicule; and trust me there have been many worthy of ridicule. She brings out the best in me and our three children, Kelsey, Daniel and Jillian. Whatever our children achieve in life will be because of their mother's dedication and love. Dee gave up her career in nursing to be a full-time mom. Our children are so much better because of her sacrifice.

Dee has a long battle ahead of her as she fights Parkinson's disease. In her honor, part of the profits of this book will be donated to the Michael J. Fox Foundation. I have always wanted to write a book, and through her support, encouragement and love; I finally have.

My parents and siblings have also been amazing to me. My father was a wonderful man, great sense of humor and hardworking. I like to think I got his best traits. My mother was nothing short of spectacular. She raised six children in a one bathroom house on my father's paycheck. We never went without a necessity and all received a private education. My mother is one of the smartest women I have ever met. I hope I received half of her common sense and IQ.

My siblings, Thomas, Gerry, Mariann, Marge and Pat all gave me unique gifts. Growing up in a big family/small house taught me how to get along with people, among many other blessings. I thank them all for their love and support over the years.

This book is dedicated to the family and friends I have been blessed to know. A special thanks to Bill Clark and Scott Nelson, two friends I can always count on. I hope that this book helps others prepare for their retirement. The state of our country's finances is uncertain, at best. It would be unwise to bank on social security to provide for our financial needs in retirement. With the lessons in this book, I hope every reader becomes better ready to retire, and retire in style!

Last but not least, how could I forget Riley, our beagle? Thanks for always listening!

About the Author

Hugh W. Connelly is managing member of Independent Retirement Advisers, LLC ("IR Advisers"), a NJ-based investment adviser. Frustrated with his own 401K plan, he founded IR Advisers to help people to take better advantage of their 401K retirement plans.

Hugh has investment management experience and has worked as an investment banker in the asset securitization realm. His experience also includes commercial banking which experience includes syndicating multi-bank revolving credit facilities, international lending in multi-currencies, commercial paper conduits, asset securitization, and investment banking. He founded the internet leasing company VerticaLease.com, as well as small ticket lessors FirstLease, Inc. and Vanguard Leasing, Inc. He's the managing editor of The Main Street Herald (www.MainStreetHerald.com), a small business blog.

Hugh's academic credentials are of the highest quality. A chartered financial analyst (CFA) charter holder—the premier financial certification, awarded by the CFA Institute—Hugh holds a bachelor's degree from Temple University and a master of science in finance—from Drexel University. He's also a certified fund specialist (CFS), a designation awarded by the Institute of Business & Finance to finance professionals who have become experts in analyzing the nuances of mutual funds, exchange traded funds and other financial instruments.

Hugh is an adjunct professor of finance at Strayer University in Philadelphia.

Married with three children, Hugh is a British car enthusiast and an avid runner. He has completed many marathons including the New York, Philadelphia, Boston, Reykjavik, Dublin, Belfast, Rome and the original Athens Marathon in Greece.

Introduction

My parents taught me to save from an early age. Later, when I was working, my father told me to "pay yourself first." What he meant was that I should use my payroll deduction as a savings tool. That way, I could spend my paycheck without worrying that I was living beyond my means. I started with US savings bonds and then added a 401K once I was eligible to contribute. Since that time, I have always been interested in how 401Ks work. I remember questioning why my company's 401K plan mutual funds were only the funds managed by my employer, a bank. Those funds performed poorly and we all had no choice but to invest in them. Thankfully, the laws have changed and employers can't do that anymore.

I'm a knowledgeable financial professional, and yet when I would look at my 401K statements I would get frustrated about not achieving a good return, not maximizing the match, and other loopholes that kept me from maximizing the plan assets. Then amidst the market crash in 2008/2009 I got fed up with my plan going down, down, down. I didn't want to sell low, but decided I was going to change my new contributions to cash so I could at least preserve the value of new contributions until the market got better.

Pretty smart, huh? I thought so, until I got my next statement and saw that my cash balance had gone *down*!

Now what? I thought to myself. So I dug in and found out that the interest rate on the cash fund was 0.28%; nothing to write home about, but still a positive number. So why did the balance go down? Well, the "management fee" on the fund was 0.50%, so 0.28% (gain) minus 0.50% (fee deducted) meant my cash balance *lost* 0.22%. And that loss is guaranteed! That's not what I had in mind when I shifted my allocation to the safety of cash.

And then I thought, if I struggle to figure out this crap, how the heck is the average American going to? And that's when I decided to do something and create a system that anyone can follow to maximize their plan's value and stay on course for retirement. I created the 401K Tune-Up Plan because retirement funds are too important to be ignored.

I'll say it again, here and elsewhere in the book: "You can't afford to ignore it!"

My system for tuning up your 401K plan starts off with a personal risk assessment. This assessment will let you measure your personal risk profile. That's the first step in determining how you should manage your plan. Too many web calculators or other impersonal resources think the only thing that matters is your age. Not me; your personal risk profile is a big part of the plan that others ignore. In this book I cover many aspects of 401K plans from their history, plan mechanics, and how to analyze the best funds for you. I have worksheets that take you step-by-step through the fund analysis process. Every plan is different and has different investment choices, but my system is flexible and lets you use the worksheets to analyze any plan. Then once you have your risk profile and an understanding of the fund options, I show you how to maximize your employer match and rebalance the plan when appropriate.

All it takes is ten minutes four times a year—or forty minutes a year—to make sure your 401K is properly tuned to meet your needs. Your retirement is too important to ignore, and "You can't afford to ignore it!"

Here's my guarantee: if you're not 100% satisfied with the system and its results for you, simply return it to my attention within 90 days of new purchase from an authorized book seller for a 110% refund. I'm that certain that you will get value from this system. So you have no risk. Go ahead buy the 401K Tune-Up book and get started on your retirement plan today!

Program Overview

We Americans spend a lot of time and money on our cars. People who have an expensive luxury car buy premium gas, get the oil changed, keep it washed and waxed, store it in a garage to keep it out of the weather, and have the engine tuned-up regularly. In short, Americans spend a lot of time and money caring for their cars. From a financial view, a car is an asset that goes down in value the more we use it. Even if you don't use it, it still goes down in value, unless you buy a rare car and store it right away. But who can afford that?

Yet even though a car's value goes down steadily we still put money into it for care and maintenance. Here's an interesting fact: most people who have been working and contributing to a 401K plan for at least five years have the equivalent of a BMW in their 401K plan, yet they ignore it.

You can't afford to ignore it! The 401K Tune-Up Plan is going to show you how to care for, and maximize the value of, your 401K assets. All in as little time as it takes for an oil change on your car.

Think of the time and money you put into your principal asset, your home. You spend money to make it look nice, you do projects, pay for lawn care, maybe update your kitchen, or add a powder room. It's all designed to maintain and improve the value of most American's primary asset, your home. Now in today's real estate market your home may have dropped in value, but the housing market will come back. It always has and always will. The real estate debacle in the late 1980s early 1990s was devastating, but the prices did come back, and they will again. The point is that we spend time, money and effort caring for the assets we own, but ignore our retirement plans. Why?

I think it's because the plans seem complicated—and they are; because investing is foreign to most people, and therefore scary. There are so many unknowns. It's also a personal asset, one that people don't like to talk about. We think nothing of asking a mechanic friend about that noise in our engine, or a plumbing friend how to fix a leaking faucet, but most people are uncomfortable talking about money with friends. (Except those who have money, of course—that's all they talk about.)

However, I want to tell you that if you continue to ignore your 401K, you do so at your own risk!

Some of you will have to work (and work hard) well into your seventies before you can dial it back into a semi-retirement. You know the retirement dream has changed over the years.

In the 1950s through the 1980s the retirement dream was retire and travel, lounge around, and do nothing. We all know stories of people who died too soon into that definition of retirement. But just like the American Dream, the Retirement Dream has changed too. Now, the retirement dream is to get out of the "rat race" and do something else for less money and less stress so long as it includes a health plan. Is being a Wal-Mart greeter your vision of retirement? How about sailing around the world? Or would you like to go back to school, develop a secret interest, or even teach?

Regardless of your retirement dream, you need to pay attention to your 401K plan assets.

This is not a get rich quick scheme. Investing is a marathon not a sprint. And trust me, I know about marathons—I've completed over twenty throughout the US and abroad. A marathon is all about training and efficiency. The top marathon runners of the world are not jacked. They're not six-foot-two, two-hundred-ten-pound muscular athletes. They are average in stature, thin in build and graceful in how they move. They are efficient. I want to help you in your 401K marathon to retirement. You can't get rich quick with a 401K. That's not what they are designed for, but you can get rich slow, and that's what we'll strive for.

In this book I am going to show you how. It's not difficult and my system will deliver the results. The 401K Tune-Up Plan is going to help you understand your plan and how to best manage it for you and your risk tolerance.

Remember in the old days when car maintenance took all day? You dropped the car off for service and picked it up the next day. Then came companies like Jiffy Lube, in and out in ten minutes or it's free! Remember that offer? I don't think they still have that offer but ever since then, oil changes are now much faster. That's my goal for you with this book. To give you the tools to do a ten-minute tune-up once a quarter and keep your 401K plan working and maximizing your results. That's all it takes—ten minutes, four times a year. You have the ability, I am going to give you the tools but you must invest the time. All I ask is that you work the system and invest forty minutes a year! Will you do that for me? Will you do it for yourself? In the time it takes to do an oil change, you can tune your 401K and sleep better at night with the confidence that you do understand how the plan works, how the investments are balanced, and when it's time to implement changes.

This program is not only for 401K plans. Many other investment options are 401K look-a-likes in they way they operate. Individual retirement accounts (IRAs) are a good example. In most cases IRA assets are invested in mutual funds. The techniques you learn in my system will enable you to better understand and manage IRA assets. The same is true for Coverdell Education accounts, and especially for 529 plans used to save for college. So while the name 401K Tune-Up might suggest it only applies to 401K plans, you'll get far more benefit from the program than simply how to better manage your 401K assets. Any investment that uses mutual funds or exchange traded funds will now be more easily understood, and better managed by you.

Now, here's my guarantee. I guarantee that after reading this book and implementing the system you will be more in charge of your plan assets and your performance will improve. If after using the techniques outlined in this book for ninety days you're not fully satisfied, I'll refund 110% of your new purchase price from an authorized book seller. That's how confident I am that this system works. And you get to keep the personal risk assessment for your trouble. That alone is worth the price of the book. So what are you waiting for? Another crash, the next boom? C'mon take action and stop ignoring your 401K. You can't afford to ignore it!

Chapter 1

Retirement Plan Background

How do you start? Start with the end in mind.

The first step in retirement planning is planning to retire. The earlier you start the less painful it will be. Americans spend billions of dollars a year on dieting, physical fitness, vitamins and supplements, and of course car maintenance. Yet one of the most important assets in our lives, namely our retirement, gets little attention. People will spend a small fortune on some diet drug that claims to allow them to eat whatever they want but keeps them thin and trim. To me dieting has always been a very simple process: calories in minus calories burned equals weight gain or weight loss. If you consume a lot of calories and live a sedentary lifestyle you will get fat! It's a mathematical certainty. If you eat healthy and live a moderately active lifestyle you will not get fat. That too, is a mathematical certainty. So why are people so confused by their weight? If you're overweight it's because you eat too much. The answer is easy. Stop eating and start burning calories.

Retirement planning is similarly described. If during your forty-year working career you lived paycheck to paycheck and put nothing aside for retirement you will either work until you die or retire in poverty. This too, is a mathematical certainty. The key to a long and successful retirement is to live beneath your means while working, so that you can live at your means when retired.

This book is not going to tell you how much you need to save or little tricks on where you can save a penny here or a dollar there. Rather, this book is for disciplined responsible working adults who wish to retire comfortably when they can afford to. My goal in writing this book is to help you save wisely, save smartly, then save efficiently through your employer-sponsored 401K plan. Bookstores are littered with various financial planning books, programs and software tools.

The problem with all of this information is that it completely neglects the single most important retirement asset—your 401K plan. There are almost sixty million Americans with some $3.7 trillion invested in 401K and 403B retirement savings plans. The vast majority of this money is invested in mutual funds inside your 401K or 403B plan. However, no one ever stops to think about how these plans work and how efficient or inefficient the investment choices within the plans truly are. I would hate to see someone who has been saving responsibly over their entire life have to work an additional ten years because they were not saving efficiently within their employer-sponsored plan. The lessons in this book, if followed, will help to prevent that from happening to you.

In the subsequent pages and chapters of this book I'll explain in plain English how the plans work, how mutual funds work, how to pick the winners and avoid the losers within your plan, and how to stay on track through periodic rebalancing of your investments so that you get the most out of your money. Once you read through the book and go through the process once you will see is not very difficult to review your plan in subsequent periods and make corrective changes so that you can retire on time with enough money to be comfortable. You just need to start with the end in mind.

So what will your retirement be like? Are you saving for retirement? It used to be that retirement meant not working, doing some traveling, and enjoying yourself. However, that definition of retirement seems to be fading for most people these days. Today, many people are just hoping their retirement means they can get off the "treadmill" and maybe just do some part-time job for little extra money and medical benefits. The idea here being a low stress job with medical benefits can top off insufficient retirement income. Whatever your definition of retirement is, if you participate in an employer-sponsored retirement savings plan this book will become invaluable to you. The simple lessons in this book once applied regularly will save you tens of thousands of dollars and help you achieve a more satisfactory retirement.

History of retirement plans

There was a time when virtually every company offered its employees a pension plan. They were called "defined benefit pension plans." And they were what their name suggests. After so many years of service, and attaining a certain age, workers would be eligible to retire with full pension benefits. Often times this meant a pension equal to 65% to 75% (sometimes even more!) of your pre-retirement income. You didn't have to pay for this. You didn't have to manage the investments of the pension plan. Your employer did all of this for you. Whatever its cost, you were unaware of it, and your employer picked up the tab.

By some estimates this "tab" was running approximately ten percent of payroll. That's a fairly significant cost for something somewhat intangible in the minds of today's workers—a pension plan. Nonetheless, many employers used their pension plan to attract and retain the best employees.

After years of funding pension obligations for their employees, some pension funds had grown quite large. When some sponsoring companies found themselves in need of cash they could not resist the temptation to raid the pension fund, exchanging pension cash for company notes and securities. However, when this strategy failed and these same companies went bankrupt, the pensioners found their pension plans had insufficient assets to pay pension benefits. The plans failed and the pensioner's lives were ruined.

In response the US government stepped in and passed laws protecting pension plans and preventing companies from raiding them. At around the same time the accountants started to put pen to paper and measure whether or not pension plans were adequately funded given the pension liability they owed to retirees. When the stock market went up, the pension plans would be overfunded. When stock prices went down, pension plans would be underfunded. This is because a pension plan's liabilities—the amount of money it needs to pay pensions to retirees—does not change much. The pension liability goes gradually up or down with the number of plan participants and the benefit payout rate. So, when the much more volatile stock portfolio rises, assets are greater than liabilities and the plan has excess assets. It is overfunded. Conversely, in a down stock market the pension investment portfolio goes down. The liabilities may not change and so from the accounting formula for capital (assets minus liabilities equals capital) we see the plan's "capital" falls and the plan is underfunded.

With pensions, the government will not allow pension plans to become too underfunded; and so the sponsoring company (the employer) must add more money to the plan through an expense called "pension benefit expense." This would result in a big expense that would impact profitability. This system infused companies with market risk beyond the risk of their own business. A company could be having a terrific year, financially speaking, but because of a dip in the stock market they had to add more pension assets and thus report a lower net income than the core business would suggest. As a result, many employers sought an alternative to the defined benefit pension plan.

Birth of the 401K plan

In 1978, Congress decided that Americans needed a bit of encouragement to save more money for retirement. They thought that if they gave people a way to save for retirement while at the same time lowering their state and federal taxes, they might just take advantage of it. As a result, Congress passed the Tax Reform Act. In that law, a relatively obscure part—Section 401, paragraph K—authorized a tax break for deferred income.

In financial publications you'll see it referred to as 401K or 401k, and in this book as 401K. They're all the same.

Ted Benna, who at that time was a benefits consultant, is credited with devising the first version of a retirement plan designed to use IRS Section 401, paragraph K as the basis for company-sponsored retirement accounts. His plan was officially accepted by the IRS, and proposed regulations were issued in 1981. In 1982, taxpayers were able to take advantage of this new plan for the first time. It took almost ten years, but final regulations were eventually published in 1991.

The benefit of the 401K plan for employers was that it shifted the burden of investment planning from them to the employee. Employers like 401Ks because they do not have the large pension expense, nor the financial management and record keeping responsibilities of a defined benefit plan.

In addition, they could get the employee to explicitly contribute to the retirement plan, thereby reducing the employer's total cost. Employers liked the shift from a defined *benefit* (pension) to a defined *contribution* (401K). That way they could control their pension costs.

The popularity of mutual funds coincided with the birth of 401K plans, and the two have been intertwined ever since. However, the burden of funding and managing the retirement assets has now completely shifted from the employer to the employee. Many employers offer sophisticated fund choices, which instead of helping the employees actually hurt them because the investment choices are not clearly explained. It becomes confusing and overwhelming.

Many times employees say the last time they made a change to their plan was when they got hired and established their investment choices and contribution amounts as part of the hiring packet. This investment strategy of "set-it-and-forget-it" simply doesn't work for the long term. In order to get the full value of your retirement funds you need to actively manage the plan.

I'm not talking about active management in the context of a broker constantly trading stocks. I mean you need to be active in the management of the assets in the plan. That means making deliberate choices as to which funds to invest in, not chasing funds that had strong performance last quarter. You can't chase performance.

Reversion to the Mean

The development of mathematics has continued since the dawn of man. Some of history's greatest mathematicians came from antiquity. People such as Archimedes, Pythagoras, Euclid, Sir Isaac Newton and many others have contributed greatly to the science of mathematics. However it was not until the modern era when behavior mathematics was born. Sir Francis Galton is credited with the invention of standard deviation, correlation and regression. In a now famous lecture to the Royal Institution in London, Galton first described his findings which evolved into the theory of regression to the mean.

"It is some years since I made an extensive series of experiments on the produce of seeds of different size but of the same species. They yielded results that seemed very noteworthy, and I used them as the basis of a lecture before the Royal Institution on February 9th, 1877. It appeared from these experiments that the offspring did not tend to resemble their parent seeds in size, but to be always more mediocre than they—to be smaller than the parents, if the parents were large; to be larger than the parents, if the parents were very small.

The point of convergence was considerably below the average size of the seeds contained in the large bagful I bought at a nursery garden, out of which I selected those that were sown, and I had some reason to believe that the size of the seed towards which the produce converged was similar to that of an average seed taken out of beds of self-planted specimens.

The experiments showed further that the mean filial regression towards mediocrity was directly proportional to the parental deviation from it."

Galton painstakingly studied seed size and observed in nature a natural mathematical fact, reversion to the mean. You may ask, "How does this relate to investing?" It is vital! What this means for investing is that over time, fund performance will revert to the mean (or average) level of the market return. So, by chasing the high fliers you could be dooming yourself to perpetual underperformance as these funds revert to the mean market returns. That is why index funds with low fees are such a good investment. You do not have to worry about reversion to the mean, when your investment tracks mean performance.

You also should not be taking unnecessary risk, either, by investing in risky assets as you get close to retirement age. Never bet the farm!

Rather, understand your risk profile.

I'm going to give every reader a free copy of a personal risk assessment tool. Once you understand your risk tolerance you can then start thinking about what funds to invest in. The goal is to have a diversified pool of investments. But you do have to be a little careful.

Emergence of mutual funds

Every mutual fund prospectus describes the fund's objectives, but also allows for flexibility of the fund manager. The flexibility afforded to fund managers is how fund managers attempt to beat the indexes that they are compared against. They may overweight a sub-sector of the associated index if they feel that this sub-sector will outperform the other sub-sectors in the index. This is how they beat the averages; otherwise they would always underperform the averages due to their management fees. What I mean by this is that if a fund manager exactly matched the holdings of an index they would underperform against this index by the amount of their management fee. So, some funds may not be exactly what you think they are, based solely on the fund name.

The 2012 IPO (Initial Public Offering) of Facebook is a great example. Well over 150 mutual funds and exchange traded funds "Liked" shares of Facebook when it went public in May 2012. While some may have wished they hadn't, some who did were curious buyers. Facebook is a high growth, non-dividend paying, speculative technology company, at least when it went public. What it evolves into has yet to be determined. However, some mutual fund buyers did not appear to be likely acquirers.

According to The Wall Street Journal and Morningstar, some surprising funds bought blocks of Facebook stock. A select few are listed in the table below, but there were many others.

Fund	Shares Bought	Why purchase was surprising
Fidelity Dividend Growth	167,400	Facebook does not pay a dividend.
Principal LargeCap Value	124,749	Facebook is considered a growth stock, not a value one.
Oppenheimer Main Street	1,498,530	Funds for average investors are not commonly known to invest in speculative IPOs.

Also, some funds have different names but end up with similar holdings in their top ten. So by investing in two funds designed to create diversification, you end up with concentrated risk. For example, many large funds hold similar stocks like Apple, Exxon, Chevron, or Google.

The final piece of the puzzle is to understand the management fees charged.

It is fair to pay a fund manager for his/her services. The key is to pay them fairly.

So, we all agree we need to take some risk if we expect our investments to outpace inflation and grow. But how much and what kinds?

Putting all of your contributions into cash may sound safe. With the rationale that my employer matches 50% of my contribution, I'm guaranteed a 50% return on my investment. However, as we already know investing in cash may not be a "safe" investment due to management expenses. Secondly, investing your retirement funds in cash alone is not going to allow your funds to grow sufficiently to protect you from inflation, or to enable you to retire comfortably. You might as well bury your cash in the ground.

Mutual fund management

Mutual funds are created by investment management companies whose research suggests that there is demand for a particular investment sector. In the beginning, it was simply a matter of having mutual funds that invested in the overall market.

The next question was *which* market. Some mutual funds followed the S&P 500 index. Others would follow the Dow Jones Industrial Average. As the market for stocks and bonds grew, so too did the number of indexes against which managers would be compared. There would be small-cap indexes, large-cap indexes, mid-cap, growth, value, international, and on and on.

Once the indexes had been saturated, market research suggested that investors wanted access to specific narrow sectors within the economy. That gave rise to an explosion in mutual fund choices. Today, there are literally thousands of mutual funds for an investor to choose from. Each fund manager—who essentially acts as the quarterback of the mutual fund—strives to find some area of uniqueness or differentiation that makes its fund more desirable than another. The primary way fund managers can achieve such differentiation is through performance.

But the question is, fund performance as compared to what?

Mutual funds that outperform their index or peer group get higher rankings relative to other funds. This higher ranking creates the perception of superior fund management. And superior fund management is what every investor craves.

Fund managers want to have their funds in favor with investors because of how fund managers are compensated. Fund managers are paid a management fee on the aggregate assets under management, or AUM. The bigger the fund, the more management income that is available for the fund managers. So in order to increase demand for a fund, the fund manager needs to find ways to demonstrate his or her superiority. Sometimes that's just a matter of good old-fashioned stock selection. These fund managers truly do demonstrate consistent effective superior performance when compared to their peers.

However, some fund managers cheat.

There are many ways a fund manager can beat his peers and/or the index.

First, the obvious answer is by superior stock selection.

Second is by comparing herself with an index that is not quite representative of his/her stated investment philosophy. In this way a fund manager whose style may not exactly match the goals of a particular index can appear to be a superior fund manager.

Lastly, mutual fund managers can benefit from "style creep." Style creep is where you deviate from your stated investment philosophy ever so slightly in order to take on additional risk and drive relative performance when compared to a particular index or style benchmark.

I've recently looked at the composition of Vanguard Growth Index stock mutual fund. When I looked at the top ten holdings and did a cursory review of those stocks vis-à-vis standard growth or value metrics, I was not surprised to see evidence of style creep. When you're buying a growth fund you don't expect to see value stocks in the top ten holdings, but sometimes that's exactly what you see as the fund manager reaches for results that will enable him or her to beat the index.

The Vanguard Growth fund listed the following stocks in its top holdings:

Ticker	Company Name	P/E	Dividend Yield
MCD	McDonald's	16	3.08%
UNP	Union Pacific Railroad	14	2.76%
MSFT	Microsoft	14	3.40%

The definitions of growth and value are not precisely defined nor universally accepted. However, most investors would view the above sticks as mature value stocks instead of high growth ones.

For the average fund manager who is unwilling to deviate from the index and wants to simply play it safe, his or her only option is to pay a higher sales commission to attract money to their fund. The reason some investment advisers recommend certain mutual funds is because the funds they recommend are called "institutional" shares. The unsuspecting client thinks that he/she is getting access to insider or extremely well-managed mutual funds because of the "institutional" label. In fact, it usually means these funds pay high upfront commissions to the investment managers who sell them.

I first became aware of this practice several years ago when my wife inherited some money from her father's IRA account. My father-in-law had mentioned to me before he died that funds in his IRA would be bequeathed to his daughters. He mentioned to me that he hoped this money would be used to further the education of his grandchildren. I don't know why, but he never mentioned that to his daughters or any of the other sons-in-law. So when the time came and he did pass away, my wife inherited one quarter of her father's IRA. The IRA was held at a prestigious New York investment house. When I contacted the investment adviser and told him of my and my wife's decision to invest this money for the education of our children in a 529 plan, he said he would get back to me with some recommendations, but that the New Jersey State 529 plan would *not* be among them. In his opinion the New Jersey plan, which at the time was managed by the New Jersey state treasurer's office, was a horrible plan and not a suitable investment.

I appreciated his insight and said I would rely on his recommendation as to what we chose to do. However, I was reminded of the quote from President Ronald Reagan as it related to the Soviet Union's commitment to reducing nuclear weapons: "Trust, but verify."

So I decided to do a little research of my own.

Sure enough, the New Jersey 529 plan was in fact horrible. (Several years later, the plan would be changed and professional fund managers would take over for the New Jersey state treasurer's office. However, the plan is still lacking today, in my opinion.)

Anyway, when I got the investment adviser's recommendations I was surprised to see he recommended the Alabama Institutional 529 program. Nothing against Alabama, but I was very surprised that after a thorough fifty-state analysis this particular New York-based investment adviser chose the State of Alabama's 529 plan to secure the educational needs of my children.

I asked him if he would send me copies of the fund prospectus so I could learn for myself why this fund was so desirable. He reluctantly agreed to send me the funds prospectus, but he also included an application so I could "get the ball rolling."

That made me suspicious, and so I got the prospectus online myself that very night. While not shocked at what I found, I was certainly surprised at the handsome fees the State of Alabama's Institutional 529 program permitted to be paid to investment advisers.

I was so angry at learning this that I called the adviser got him on the phone and reamed him out. At that time I had recently completed a master of science in finance. I told him I read the prospectus and did not appreciate the high fees paid to him. I then proceeded to systematically withdraw the money out of the 529 and into the New York State 529 plan. This plan does not charge an upfront fee, had very low fund fees, and was linked with a program called U-Promise. This program allowed us to register credit cards of friends and family and every time they used their card for certain purchases additional deposits were to be made into our program.

Now that's what I call a program that works for me and not for the financial adviser. Another plus of this plan was that it offered Vanguard funds as its investment options. These funds are famous for their low fees.

With my education, I had the advantage of understanding of how mutual funds work when this life experience took place. I wondered how many unsuspecting but well intentioned people simply filled out the forms the adviser sent and would find out twenty years later they didn't save enough for college for their children. Certainly they would blame themselves for not saving enough rather than the investment adviser for not giving them better advice. Plus, with the turnover in the investment advisory field it's very likely the investment adviser would be off doing something else, having earned his commissions long ago from this particular recommendation.

That was really the first time that I realized someone needed to provide independent advice on how mutual funds work and how best to compare them.

It was around this time that I learned of the new company called Morningstar. Morningstar was to be a mutual fund rating company that would create a rating that embodied a fund's performance, risk, fees, and fund manager tenure, among other things. My hope was that these Morningstar ratings would add to the transparency of the mutual fund industry, and I believe they have. But the fund ratings aren't everything, and there is still much to learn about how mutual funds work.

In the mid-1970s, during the Watergate crisis, the insider at the White House who became referred to as "Deep Throat" told reporter Robert Woodward that in order to find the answers he sought, he needed to "follow the money." And so in the next chapter, in order to find the answers to mutual funds we'll follow the money. And you will see just how much money there is to be made in the mutual fund business. Although it may sound daunting, it's not all that complicated, and I will help you see the forest through the trees in order that you may select the best mutual funds for you and your investment needs.

Chapter 2

Fee Disclosure

As we know, employees who participate in 401K plans assume all the responsibility for their retirement income. This responsibility includes making contributions as a part of their salary and by directing their own investments.

We also know that those who direct their own investments need to consider the investment objectives, risk and reward, and the overall performance of their fund choices offered in their plan.

However, until recently a large part of your fund performance was beyond your knowledge or ability to influence—namely, the fund fees. Fees and expenses are one of the factors that can dramatically impact your actual investment performance when compared to market indices.

As a result, the US Department of Labor Employee Benefits Security Administration passed a law (29 CFR Part 2550, RIN 1201-AB08) requiring fee disclosure to plan fiduciaries and participants. This law was originally to go into effect on July 16, 2011. However, based on an uproar from the mutual fund industry, this implementation date was delayed from July 16, 2011 to April 1, 2012.

So beginning in the summer of 2012 plan participants should have started to see fee disclosure information along with their quarterly 401K plan statements. This information is supposed to be clear and enable plan participants to use this data to make better investment choices. However, as you can imagine many people were confused by this additional information, especially because no one explained to the plan participants what this means or how to interpret the data.

At about the same time this fee disclosure law was coming down from the Department of Labor, a complementary ruling occurred (29 CFR Part 2550, RIN 1201-AB35). According to the Department of Labor, this ruling under the Employee Retirement Income Security Act, and parallel provisions of the Internal Revenue Code of 1986, related to the provision of investment advice to participants and beneficiaries in individual account plans, such as 401K plans. This ruling became effective on December 27, 2011.

What AB35 did was to prohibit plan fiduciaries from rendering investment advice to plan participants regarding investments that triggered the payment of additional advisory and other fees to the fiduciaries or their affiliates.

Responding to the need to afford participants greater access to professional investment advice, Congress amended the prohibited transaction provisions of ERISA and the Code, as part of the Pension Protection Act of 2006 (PPA), to permit a broader array of investment advice providers to offer their services to participants.

To make things even more complicated, these requirements are met only if the advice is provided by a fiduciary adviser under an, "eligible investment advice arrangement." There are only two general types of eligible arrangements. One is based on compliance with a "fee leveling" requirement (imposing limitations on fees and compensation of the fiduciary adviser). The other is based on compliance with a "computer model" requirement (requiring use of a certified computer model).

Well, are you confused yet?

What this ruling by the Department of Labor effectively did was require plan fees to be *disclosed* but not necessarily *understood* by the plan participants who pay them. To correct this, they then permitted plan fiduciaries (employers) to offer plan participants appropriate investment advice. The problem is that the advice of an adviser paid by the fund company whose funds they would recommend doesn't sound right to me—how about you? Do you think such advisers would point out the high fees their funds charge? I doubt it. However, to hire your own personal adviser can be expensive. Advisers generally don't want to be bothered with the smaller balances beyond their control in a 401K plan, and employers don't want to pay the cost either.

Financial advisers seek high net worth people with large portfolios. Advisers are compared and ranked by Assets Under Management, or "AUM". The bigger an investment advisory firm's AUM, the more prestigious they appear and the better the talent they can attract because of the large portfolios available for investing. Advisers cannot take 401K plan assets from outside of the employer plan while you work there. They cannot add to their AUM by advising 401K plan participants. So they do not target small middle class investors with comparatively small investment portfolios most of which is inside a 401K plan.

Your other option is a computer model. The problem with the computer model is that it is by definition impersonal and does not ensure that the plan participant actually understands what the model is telling them to do.

So what is a plan participant or an employer to do? The answer is to make sure that plan participants receive proper education about retirement planning, mutual funds, and asset allocation. This way the plan participants are not just following a blind model that may or may not be suitable for them. Rather, they are actually educated about investing and empowered to control their own plan assets and thereby their own destiny. This is what the 401K Tune-Up Plan offers you—education, freedom, and confidence to retire in style.

Chapter 3

Dissecting a Mutual Fund

How fund managers make money

A mutual fund is a basket of stocks selected by a fund manager. This portfolio of stocks will determine the fund's performance.

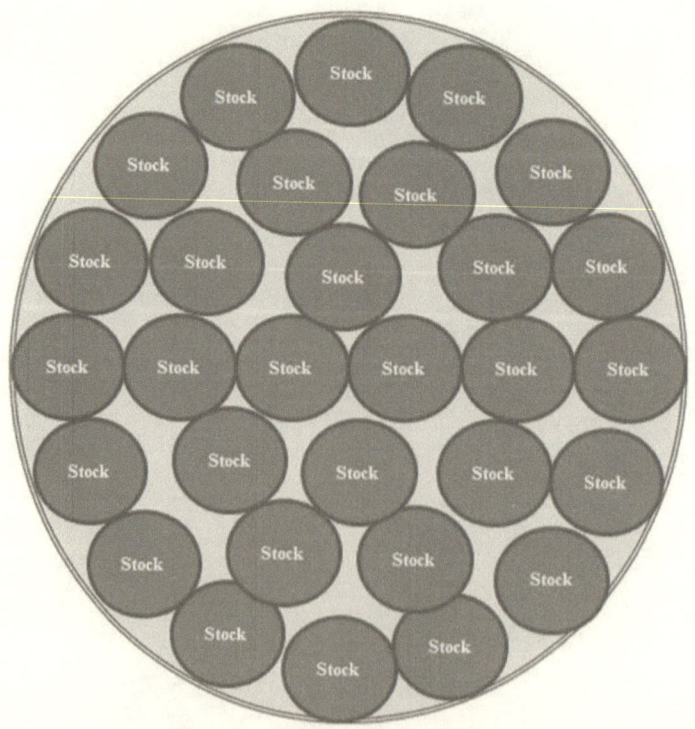

401K Plan fees

As previously discussed, more and more employees are investing their futures through 401K plans. The days when you could count on your employer and their pension plan to provide for your retirement are gone. Employees who participate in 401K plans assume responsibility for their retirement income by deferring part of their salary and by directing their own investment choices. You may not think much about the responsibility of directing your own investment choices, but it's a serious responsibility too few people pay enough attention to. As we will expand upon in the next chapter, this responsibility includes not just proper funds selection but also appropriate asset allocation.

For those of you who direct your own investment selections without the help of professional advice, in order to make sound investment decisions you'll need to pay particular attention to each fund's investment objectives, the risk and return characteristics, and the performance over time of each investment option offered by your plan. It's not good enough to simply select a stock or bond fund. You must select the best stock or bond fund, and that means understanding fund fees. Fees and expenses are one of the big factors that will determine your investment returns and ultimately your retirement lifestyle.

In this chapter, I'll answer some common questions about various fee types and expenses that may be paid by your 401K plan. I highlight the most common fees, and enable you to make informed investment decisions, consider fees as a critical part of your decision-making process, compare the costs and services, realize that past performance is no guarantee of future performance, and realize that the most expensive funds aren't always the best performers.

Why should you care about plan fees?

In a 401K plan, the balance in your account when you retire will determine what kind of retirement you have. While you can maximize your current contributions and company match, fees and expenses paid by the plan can substantially erode the growth in your plan assets. The table below offers an example of a thirty-year-old earning $30,000 a year who plans to retire thirty-five years later, at age sixty-five.

In scenario 1, the thirty-five-year average gross return of her plan assets was nine percent. She selected low-cost index funds and had fees and expenses of only fifty basis points. That left her an average net return of

8.5%. Assuming no further contributions were made her fund balance would grow to a retirement value of over $520,000.

In scenario 2, the same plan assets only grow to $377,000 despite earning the same average gross return. The difference of $144,000 is attributed to higher fees and expenses by 100 basis points. Although it may not sound like much, fees higher by just one percent can reduce your retirement assets by as much as 28% over your working horizon. This is a substantial reduction in plan assets that would have a material negative effect on your lifestyle in retirement. In fact, it may even cause you to delay retirement because you may not have sufficient assets on which to live.

If you get nothing else from this book you must pay attention to fees and expenses from the mutual funds you select out of your 401K plan. If you ignore fund fees and expenses, you do so at your own risk.

		Scenario 1	Scenario 2
Current Balance	$	30,000	$ 30,000
Current Age		30	30
Retirement Age		65	65
Years until Retirement		35	35
Investment Return		9.00%	9.00%
LESS: Fees		0.50%	1.50%
Net Invetsment Return		8.50%	7.50%
Future Value	$	521,389	$ 377,066
Variance in Dollars:	$	144,323	
Variance as %		28%	

You should also be aware that your employer has a specific obligation to consider the fees and expenses paid by your plan. ERISA requires employers to follow certain rules while managing 401K plans. Employers are held to a high standard of care and diligence and must administer their duties solely in the interest of plan participants and their beneficiaries. According to the US Department of Labor, employers must:

- Establish a proven process for selecting investment alternatives and service providers;
- Ensure that fees paid to service providers and other expenses of the plan are reasonable in light of the level and quality of services provided;
- Select investment alternatives that are prudent and adequately diversified; and
- Monitor investment alternatives and service providers once selected to see that they continue to be appropriate choices.

What are the plan fees?

401K plan fees and expenses generally fall into three categories.

1. Plan administration fees. These fees and expenses represent the costs of providing basic administrative services such as plan record keeping, accounting, legal and trustee services that are required in order to administer a 401K plan. Most 401K plans also offer a host of additional services such as Web access, telephone voice response access, access to customer service representatives; educational seminars, retirement planning software, and other forms of plan benefits.

Some of the costs of administrative services will be covered by investment fees that are deducted from investment returns. Otherwise, if administrative costs are separately charged, they will be born either by your employer or charged directly against the assets of the plan. When paid directly by the plan, administrative fees are either allocated among individual accounts in proportion to each account balance or passed through as a flat fee against each participant's account. Either way, the more services provided the higher the fees.

2. Investment choice fees. Without a doubt the largest component of 401K plan fees and expenses is associated with managing plan investments. Fees for investment management and other investment related services generally are assessed as a percentage of assets invested. These are the fees that can destroy a retirement plan's assets. You pay for these costs in the form of an indirect charge against your account because they're deducted directly from your investment returns. Your net total return is your return after these fees have been paid.

3. Individual service fees. In addition to the overall administrative expenses, there may be individual service fees associated with optional features offered under a 401K plan. These kinds of fees are related to discretionary services that an individual may choose to use. If you never use the services, you never pay any of these fees. An example of the typical individual service fee is a fee charged to a participant for taking the loan from the plan. Many plans charge an admin fee to set up a loan. However, if you never borrow from your plan assets you won't have to pay these fees.

Regardless of the type of fee, plan fees need to be evaluated and measured in the context of the service provided to be sure there is fair value for the money paid. It is the employer's responsibility to see that this is the case. However, in my opinion, not enough attention is paid in adequately analyzing plan fees in relation to the plan benefits.

401K investment choice fees

Most 401K plans today offer mutual funds, variable annuities, or company stock as the investment vehicles a plan participant can choose from. While still somewhat rare today, exchange traded funds or ETFs are gaining ground against mutual funds because of their low cost and efficiency. In this section, I'll focus on mutual funds and variable annuities as well as their associated fees.

Mutual funds

Mutual funds pool and invest the money of many people. Each investor owns shares in a mutual fund that represent a part of the mutual funds aggregate holdings. The portfolio securities held by mutual fund is managed by a professional investment adviser following the specific investment policy. Mutual funds make money by charging various fees to the fund investors. These dollar fees are normally converted into percentage points and measured as a percentage of plan assets. In that way, very large mutual funds have a pricing advantage, as they only need to charge a few basis points on plan assets to generate substantial amounts of revenue for the mutual fund management company. In addition to fund management fees, some funds also charge these fees:

Loads. Some funds charge front-end loads when you make an initial investment in a fund. A front-end load is nothing more than a sales charge associated with buying a fund. The front-end load usually comes right off the top of your investment, so that the amount of your dollars that go to work are curtailed.

For example, suppose you invested $100 a month into a mutual fund with a 5% front-end load. Each month, the fund management company would collect your $100, deduct its $5 front-end load, and invest the remaining $95 into plan assets.

Some funds charge back-end loads, sometimes called a deferred sales charge or redemption fee. This is the opposite of the front-end load. With back-end loads the fee is deducted when you sell your fund assets and is often linked to how long you own plan assets. Many times a fund prospectus will describe the back-end load as a means to deter early sales of funds. Here the fund manager is trying to trap you into the fund by assessing a fee against your plan assets if you choose to get out early.

I would never invest in any fund that charged either a front-end or back-end load. There just are simply too many other good mutual funds out there to choose from that do not charge these fees. If you find a mutual fund in your 401K plan that charges either of these fees ask your human resources representative why.

Rule 12 B-1 fees. Mutual funds are allowed by law to charge plan participants for the fund's ongoing advertising, marketing, commissions, and costs of promoting the fund to investors. These fees provide no real benefit to fund investors. They are simply another means for fund managers to pass along their overhead to the plan participants. While these fees are legal and well disclosed, I can never recommend investing in any fund that charges 12 B-1 fees. These fees are usually between 0.25% and 1% of assets annually. These fees alone can destroy your retirement dreams over a thirty-five—to forty-year work horizon. And you get no economic benefit at all for these fees and expenses. I strongly urge you to avoid any fund that charges 12 B-1 fees. If you have an investment adviser who recommends 12 B-1 fees it's probably because his commissions are paid out of these fees. Do not pay twice for the same investment advice. If you pay for investment advice, ask if the adviser gets any commission or other income from the investment company whose investments he or she recommends. At least this way if you're paying twice, you'll know it.

No-load funds. This fund category came about in reaction to competition from load funds. But a no-load fund simply means that there is no front-end or back-end load or fee. Although many people mistakenly assume it also does not include any 12 B-1 fees, that is not what a no-load fund means. No-load funds are able to charge 12 B-1 fees. You'll just need to check the disclosure statement to see if that's the case or not.

Target date retirement funds. These funds have become extremely popular lately due to the perceived simplicity of funds selection. With these funds you simply select the fund that aligns with your anticipated retirement year. The theory is that the fund managers will oversee the asset allocation so that as you get closer to retirement less of the funds assets are invested in risky investments that could jeopardize your fund balance come retirement.

However, these funds can be very expensive. And part of the reason I'm writing this book is to allow you to manage your funds yourself and not have to pay extra to see that your plan assets meet your retirement needs. Different target date funds may charge different fees even if they have the same target date. The resulting layering of fees from each of the underlying mutual funds can have a compounding effect on the destructive forces of fund fees. So again, you have to look into the prospectus and see what the fund's actual costs and charges are. In addition, if the target date fund invests in other mutual funds, you'll pay fees to both the target date fund and the funds they invest in. Double the fees mean even less retirement income for you and your beneficiaries. While these funds seem intuitive and obvious, they can be very expensive fund choices. I hope that after reading this book you will not need to invest in a target date fund. You will see it is not that difficult to manage your own plan assets and the money you save may enable you to retire in style.

Fee Transparency

The Department of Labor regulations that went into effect in 2012 require plan providers to disclose the fees paid by both the employer and the employee for their 401K plans. The goal of these regulations was to clearly show plan participants the true costs of their 401K plans. The new fee disclosures were intended to help not just the employee understand the true costs of their plan, but to also help employers truly understand the real costs of providing the plan.

As plan statements went out in the summer and fall of 2012 many employees became even more confused by the vague, onerous and confusing fee disclosures. The regulations did not stipulate exactly how the fees were to be disclosed. Therefore, fee disclosure across plans is not uniform. Further, fees disclosed are not compared to any industry benchmark or other metric that would provide plan participants with some idea as to the reasonableness of their plan's fees. Some fee disclosures were not precise and only offered a range of fees. It would have been nice if the Department of Labor spelled out precise calculations that resulted in one easy to understand expense number, or percentage. However, that is not what they did and so the lobbyists of the large money management firms earned their keep.

Fee transparency was further complicated by the plan administrators. What I mean by this is that there is an inherent "agency issue" between the plan administrators goals and the goals of the employees in the plan. The plan administrators are trying to show the employer the range of services they provide, the efficient means by which they provide the services, and some indication of the economy of the services. However, their goal is not to empower employees to maximize their retirement readiness. Instead, the plan administrator's goal is to hold onto their business with the employer and not maximize the number of employees who can retire with sufficient plan assets.

We know that investment management fees can act like "termites" slowly, relentlessly eroding the long-term value of our retirement nest egg. That's why it's even more important that the Department of Labor consider amending its regulations to require clear and consistent fee disclosure calculations. The plan administrators should then go one step further and provide personalized annual statements that show the true performance of each fund owned by a plan participant, net of all fees. In addition, the fees paid by the plan should be benchmarked against industry averages to clearly highlight egregious fees.

Variable annuities

Insurance companies frequently offer a range of investment alternatives for 401K plans through a group of variable annuity contract between an insurance company and an employer on behalf of the plan. Variable annuities may include one or more insurance elements that are not present in other investment alternatives. Generally, these elements include an annuity feature, interest expense guarantees, and sometimes even a death benefit. Variable annuities can be made very complex and with complexity comes cost. In addition to investment management fees and administrative fees, variable annuities may also include these other fees:

Insurance related charges that are embedded within investment options that make disentangling the real cost of either a challenge. They include items such as sales expenses, mortality risk charges and the cost of issuing and administering contracts.

Surrender and transfer charges are fees an insurance company may charge when an employer terminates the contract before the term of the contract expires or if you withdraw an amount from the contract. This is somewhat akin to a back-end load on a regular mutual fund. This fee may be imposed if a withdrawal occurs before the expiration of the stated fund.

There is a certain appeal to variable annuity contracts because they take the investment risk and responsibility away from the investor and place it on the shoulders of the annuity issuer. However, I find these investments are usually more expensive than they are worth, and pay large commissions to the investment advisers who sell them further validating their high price, in my opinion.

A well-diversified 401K plan managed using the techniques described in this book and periodically rebalanced is the most efficient way for you to get all the benefits of your 401K plan without paying unnecessary fees to third parties. Remember, all these little fees add up, and they slowly and relentlessly erode the growth in your plan assets and reduce the amount of retirement funds available to you in retirement.

How can I get my plan's fee information?

If you have questions about the fees and expenses charged to your 401K plan, contact your human resources plan administrator who will be able to assist you with key documents.

The plan administrator should provide you with copies of documents describing investment management and other fees associated with each of the investment options available to you. This would normally be a **fund prospectus**. You also can get them directly from the fund management company, but to be sure you're looking at right numbers, first get the prospectuses from your human resources representative. Sometimes funds have different classes and the fund your plan offers may have different fees and expenses when compared to funds that the fund management company sells through brokers.

Your **account statement** will show the total assets in your account, how they are invested, and any increases or decreases in your investments during the period covered by the statement. It may also show administrative expenses charged to your account. Your plan may provide the fund's statements quarterly or annually. However if your plan offers online access you can check the plan balances at any time via the Internet. If your plan offers Internet access I strongly urge you to sign up for and get familiar with the web interface. This will enable you to become more comfortable making changes to your plan.

Your 401K plan's **summary plan description** (SPD) will tell you what the plan provides and how it operates. It may tell you that it's administrative expenses are paid by your plan rather than by your employer, and how these expenses are allocated among plan participants. A copy of the SPD is furnished to participants when they join a plan and every five years if there are material modifications or every ten years if there are no modifications.

The plan's **annual report** (Form 5500 series) contains information regarding the plan's assets, liabilities, income, and expenses, and shows the aggregate administrative fees and other expenses paid by the plan. However, it will not show if expenses deducted from investment results were fees and expenses paid by your individual account. Fees paid by your employer also will not be shown. You can receive a copy from the plan administrator. Starting with the 2009 annual reports, you can also review the report online at www.efast.dol.gov. While there is a lot of interesting information in the form 5500, it is not overly useful from the perspective of a plan participant. However, if you have an interest in learning more about your particular plan, the form 5500 can be a very informative tool. And now that they're available on the Internet, you don't have to bother human resources with the request for a copy.

The Financial Industry Regulatory Authority (FINRA) is the largest independent regulatory authority for all securities firms in the United States. FINRA's mission is to "Protect America's investors by making sure the securities industry operates fairly and honestly." They have a useful tool on their website that analyzes mutual funds, exchange traded funds and exchange traded notes. The FINRA fund analyzer report is an excellent tool to compare the expense rates of mutual funds side-by-side. Since FINRA is an independent regulatory authority it provides fair and balanced analysis of mutual funds, exchange traded funds, and exchange traded notes, all for free. The web address (at the time of this writing) is:

Go to URL: http://apps.finra.org/fundanalyzer/1/fa.aspx

Oddly enough, the analysis does not display 12b-1 fees. As previously stated, we do not believe anyone should invest in a fund that charges these advertising and distribution fees. However, it appears that the 12b-1 fees are included in the total fee calculation. It would just be nice if the fees were always broken out.

Example analysis

Next we will go through an example of how to take a quick look at similar mutual funds and determine which of the two may be better.

First, we'll go to the website listed at the bottom of the previous section. When we go to the site I enter in the mutual fund ticker symbol for my first fund. The first one that we'll analyze is the Vanguard Prime Fund investor shares (ticker symbol VPMCX). When the website finds that fund just click on it, and it will move to the right-hand column to be included in the fund analysis. Next we'll go back to the search window on the left-hand side of the page and type in the symbol for our comparison fund, the Munder Growth Opportunities Fund class A (ticker symbol MNNAX). When the fund is found we'll select it and it will join the Vanguard fund to the right. Once you have both funds shown, click on "show results." And now for the first time you will see a fair comparison of two funds you may have to choose from in your 401K plan.

The first part of the report is called the **expense analysis summary**. This part of the report will list some basic characteristics of the fund. In my example I assumed an estimated return of 8% per year and a holding period of ten years. The analysis shows the fund value after ten years, and whether or not there would be a profit or loss.

And now we get to interesting material—**total fees and sales charges**. Total fees for the Vanguard fund are $660.73. Total fees for the Munder fund are $2,959.93, which is comprised of fees of $2,409.93 and an upfront sales charge of $550.

	Vanguard PRIMECAP Fund Investors Shares	Munder Growth Opportunities Fund Class A
Data as of:	6/12/2012	6/5/2012
Ticker Symbol	VPMCX	MNNAX
Investment Amount	$ 10,000.00	$ 10,000.00
Estimated Return you selected	8.00%	8.00%
Holding Period Years	10.00	10.00
Fund Value after 10 Years	$ 20,639.36	$ 16,905.52
Profit/(Loss)	$ 10,639.36	$ 6,905.52
Total Fees and Sales Charges	$ 660.73	$ 2,959.93
Total Fees	$ 660.73	$ 2,409.93
Total Sales Charges	$ -	$ 550.00

Next we see a graph showing the value of the respective funds over ten and twenty years; and obviously, the further out we go on the time horizon the greater the variance in performance. You can just imagine someone who had the Munder fund in a 401K for twenty years and how disappointed they would be with the value come retirement, which would be a substantial variance as a percentage of assets when compared to the low-cost Vanguard PRIMECAP Fund. According to the analysis, after twenty years the Vanguard fund would be worth $42,598.32 with accumulated fees of $2,024.43. Compared with a fund value of $30,243.02 in the Munder fund, which would have charged you fees and expenses of $7,271.15. The difference in value at the end of twenty years is $12,355.30. Wouldn't you rather have that money in your account?

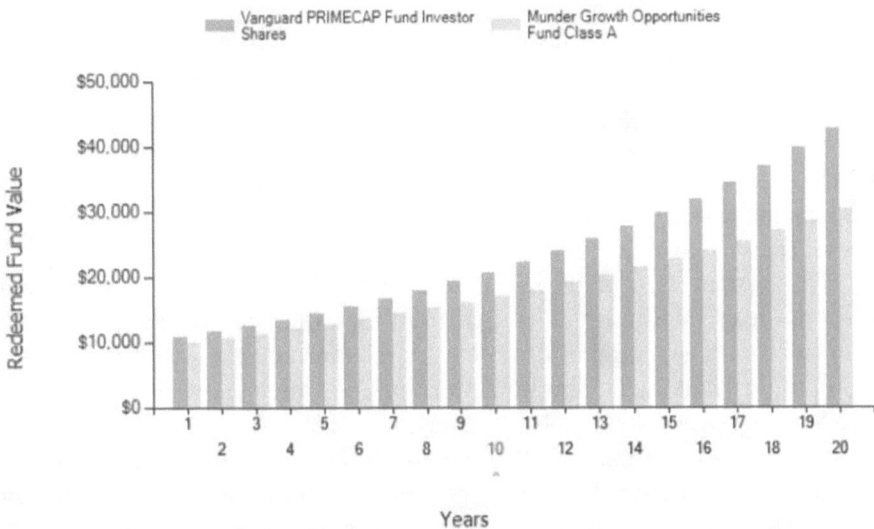

The next section of that report talks about the **annual expense comparison**. It shows the annual operating expenses for the Vanguard fund are .45%, whereas the same expense rate on the Munder fund is 1.88%. According to FINRA's analysis, the Munder fund's expenses are 417% higher than the Vanguard fund's expense rate.

Annual Expense Comparison by Product and Share Class		
	Vanguard PRIMECAP Fund Investors Shares	Munder Growth Opportunities Fund Class A
Annual Operating Expenses	0.45%	1.88%
Prospecttive Objective	Fees < Average of similar Growth Funds: 1.33%	Fees > Average of similar Growth Funds: 1.42%
Morningstar Category	Fees < Average of similar Large Growth Funds: 1.15%	Fees > Average of similar Large Growth Funds: 1.27%
Morningstar Rating (3 year)	Fees < Average of similar Morningstar Rated Funds: 1.03%	Fees > Average of similar Morningstar Rated Funds: 1.20%

The other interesting information in this fund comparison is that the report shows how these fees compared to similar funds. For example, the Vanguard fund has lower than the average amount of fees. Vanguard's average fees were .45%, while the average fees were 1.33% from the 253 mutual funds in its peer group.

It also compares this fund to the Morningstar category, where it's also lower than the average fee rate for funds in the same Morningstar category of 1.15%.

Lastly, it looks at the fees when compared to the Morningstar rating of funds rated three stars or better over a three-year period where the average is 1.03%.

So in all categories, from a fee expense standpoint, the Vanguard PRIMECAP fund has significantly lower fees. Whereas using the same three comparison categories, the Munder fund's expense ratio is substantially higher than the average fund.

The next section of the report called **fund details** gives a very nice breakdown of investment objective fund classification Morningstar rating over the last three years, it also includes the Morningstar-style box which is a proprietary ranking system from Morningstar, which makes it easy to see a fund's category and style based upon capitalization (small, mid or large) and by style (meaning value, growth or a blend of the two). It is interesting to note that while the Vanguard fund appears to perform substantially better than the Munder fund, the Munder fund has a five-star Morningstar rating.

Fund Details		
	Vanguard PRIMECAP Fund Investors Shares	**Munder Growth Opportunities Fund Class A**
Investment Objective	Growth	Growth
Ticker Symbol	VPMCX	MNNAX
Minimum Initial Purchase	$ 3,000.00	$ 2,500.00
Average Annual Return 1 Year	-7.11%	-5.04%
Average Annual Return 5 Year	1.06%	3.91%
Average Annual Return 10 Year	6.34%	9.35%
Average Annual Return Lifetime	12.66%	8.16%
Morningstar Rating 3-Year (Stars)	Three	Five

Next we get some basic information about the fund's investment sizes its actual returns and again a nice breakdown of the fees.

Then we have some additional information including **rights of accumulation** (ROA). This is a right that allows a shareholder to receive a reduced sales charge when the amount of mutual funds purchased plus the amount already held equals an ROA breakpoint. Since the Vanguard fund doesn't charge a sales charge it's not applicable. However, it is applicable on the Munder fund and the particulars are shown in the report.

The next category in the report talks about a similar sales charge issue called **letter of intent** (LOI). The LOI is a statement from an investor to the fund indicating his or her intent to invest money in the fund at an amount in excess of a sales charge breakpoint within a specified period of time. Funds with upfront sales charges need to offer their clients time to invest larger amounts in order to pay a reduced sales charge.

To me, it's just further evidence of the egregious nature of upfront sales loads. The LOI provides an investor with a way of immediately qualifying for lower sales charge assuming they meet the qualifications within the time allotted. If, however, the investor does not contribute the specified amount of funds in order to qualify for the lower sales charge when the time expires, the investor will get a bill representing the difference between the breakpoint sales charge and the amount that would've been charged without the breakpoint.

It's just more reason to avoid funds with upfront sales charge.

The next major section of the report is **contingent deferred sales charge** (CDSC). These are in essence the opposite of upfront sales charges. These are fees charged to an investor who sells his funds before a minimum holding period has been attained. The fund companies will tell you that these fees are designed to help investors resist the urge to chase performance by jumping from one fund to another. They will tell you that these funds help investors stay calm during volatile periods and enable investors to ultimately get better returns because they're not constantly jumping from fund to fund, chasing performance statistics. I'm sure this reads very nicely in their glossy fund brochures surrounded by happy smiling investors, but in my opinion CDSC fees are a means to trap investors in underperforming funds with high fees. This benefits the fund manager far more than the fund investor. I would not invest in any fund with upfront or back-end sales charges. As I have stated, there are just too many other good funds to choose from that do not charge such fees.

Although the next section of the report talks about **12 B-1 fees**, it correctly lists that the Vanguard fund does not charge such fees. However, it says it was unable to display the value for the Munder fund. However, by looking at the fund perspectives, which is linked to from this report, I was able to uncover that the 12 B-1 fees which are charged are included in the 1.88% expense fee shown earlier in this report.

Our final set of fees in this analysis is **redemption fees**. Redemption fees are more fees charged when you sell your fund. Neither of these funds have such fees.

So we have reviewed a thorough analysis of two funds using the free FINRA fund analysis tool. It should come as no surprise that the Vanguard fund has very low fees, for that is the hallmark of the Vanguard Group. I did find it interesting, however, that while the Vanguard fund appears to outperform the Munder fund over long periods of time, Morningstar gave the Munder fund five stars compared with only three stars for the Vanguard fund. To me this just shows the importance of not relying on one fund analysis method. Rather, we need to take a holistic approach to analyzing mutual funds. Normally this would be a very complex time-consuming and challenging exercise. However, the FINRA website makes this analysis far easier.

In this chapter I've given my opinion about upfront sales charges. However, to be fair I would like to also present some information directly from the Munder website which shows the effect of long holding periods on fund fees and the relative advantage of choosing the best fund class from a fee standpoint given your intended holding period. What we have below is the Munder growth opportunities fund fees by class. This information does a good job showing how different fee types can impact the aggregate amount of fees you pay based upon the mix of upfront fees, ongoing management fees, deferred sales charges, and other costs. This particular fund has five different classes of shares as shown in the table below.

MNNAX Munder Growth Opportunities A

INVESTMENT OBJECTIVE

The Fund's investment objective is to provide long-term capital appreciation.

FEES & EXPENSES OF THE FUND

The table below describes the fees and expenses that you may pay if you buy and hold shares of the Fund. You may qualify for sales charge discounts if you and your family invest, or agree to invest in the future, at least $25,000 in the Munder Funds. More information about these and other discounts is available from your financial professional and in the section entitled "Applicable Sales Charges" on page 9 of the Fund's Prospectus and the section entitled "Additional Purchase, Redemption, Exchange and Conversion "Information" on page 58 of the Statement of Additional Information.

SHAREHOLDER FEES (fees paid directly from your investment)	Class A Shares	Class B Shares	Class C Shares	Class R Shares	Class Y Shares
Maximum Sales Charge (Load) Imposed on Purchases (as a percentage of offering price)	5.50% (a)	None	None	None	None
Maximum Deferred Sales Charge (Load) (as a percentage of the lesser of original purchase price or redemption proceeds)	None (b)	5.00% c	1.00% (d)	None	None

ANNUALIZED FUND OPERATING EXPENSES (expenses that you pay each year as a percentage of the value of your investment)	Class A Shares	Class B Shares	Class C Shares	Class R Shares	Class Y Shares
Management Fee(s)	0.75%	0.75%	0.75%	0.75%	0.75%
Distribution and/or Service (12b-1) Fees	0.25%	1.00%	1.00%	0.50%	0.00%
Other Expenses	0.88%	0.89%	0.88%	0.86%	0.90%
Total Annual Fund Operating Expenses(e)	1.88%	2.64%	2.63%	2.11%	1.65%

(a) The sales charge declines as the amount invested increases.

(b) A 1.00% deferred sales charge, also known as a contingent deferred sales charge (CDSC), applies to redemptions of Class A shares within one year of purchase if purchased with no initial sales charge as part of an investment of $1 million or more and if your broker or financial intermediary received a sales commission on the purchase.

(c) A deferred sales charge, also known as a contingent deferred sales charge (CDSC), applies to redemptions of Class B shares within six years of purchase and declines over time.

(d) A deferred sales charge, also known as a contingent deferred sales charge (CDSC), applies to redemptions of Class C shares within one year of purchase.

(e) The expense information has been restated to reflect the Management Fees effective March 1, 2011.

(f) Under the Fund's Distribution Agreement, Rule 12b-1 fees are limited to 0.50% of the average daily net assets of the Fund attributable to its Class R shares.

The table above shows that class Y shares have the overall lowest total annual fund operating expenses of 1.65%. You will note that the management fee of .75% is the same regardless of which class of fund you invest in, but the other fees are much different. One might ask oneself, given the above information why would anyone invest in anything other than the class Y shares? And given the above information, a rational investor likely would choose the class Y shares; however, the investment advisers peddling these funds will likely not show you the other options and direct you toward funds with higher fees because the advisers likely get higher commissions from those funds.

Also from the website, Munder shows the effect of expenses on your investment in each of the various classes of shares. Again, you see that the class Y shares have the lowest overall fees. In another note, the fund company points out that it does not charge sales loads on reinvested dividends and other distributions reinvested in the fund. How generous of them! I've yet to find an example of a fund company that charges a sales load on reinvested dividends, but I'm sure they exist. How outrageous would that be if you were charged sales loads when you reinvested dividends into a mutual fund?

The example is intended to help you compare the cost of investing in the Fund to the cost of investing in other mutual funds. The example assumes that you invest $10,000 in the Fund for the time periods indicated and then redeem all of your shares at the end of those periods. The example also assumes that your investment has a 5% return each year and that the Fund's operating expenses remain the same. Although your actual costs may be higher or lower, based on these assumptions your costs would be:

	Class A Shares	Class B Shares	Class C Shares	Class R Shares	Class Y Shares
1 Year	$ 730	$ 767	$ 366	$ 214	$ 168
3 Years	$1,108	$1,120	$ 817	$ 661	$ 520
5 Years	$1,510	$1,599	$1,394	$1,134	$ 896
10 Years	$2,630	$2,787	$2,963	$2,442	$1,953

You would pay the following expenses if you did not redeem your shares:

	Class A Shares	Class B Shares	Class C Shares	Class R Shares	Class Y Shares
1 Year	$ 730	$ 267	$ 266	$ 214	$ 168
3 Years	$1,108	$ 820	$ 817	$ 661	$ 520
5 Years	$1,510	$1,399	$1,394	$1,134	$ 896
10 Years	$2,630	$2,787	$2,963	$2,442	$1,953

The example does not reflect sales charges (loads) on reinvested dividends and other distributions because sales charges (loads) are not imposed by the Fund on reinvested dividends and other distributions.

So that is an example of how we go through mutual funds to compare relative fees and expenses in a fair and unbiased manner to choose the fund best suited for our investment need and expense comfort level.

To review, here is how the process works:

1. Select the stock/bond mix
2. Within each category determine which sub categories you will use (for example, **stocks:** growth/income/large cap/small cap/etc. and for **bonds:** government/corporate/high quality/low quality/etc.)
3. After narrowing to the fund sub categories, then evaluate which funds in those categories you will select using the FINRA web-based mutual fund screening tool.

Morningstar

The following information was redacted from Morningstar brochures and website. "In the early 1980s, the mutual fund industry was experiencing dramatic growth. However, comprehensive information about fund performance was not readily available to individual investors. Most individuals—for whom mutual funds were created—lacked the tools they needed to track, analyze, and make intelligent decisions about mutual funds. Morningstar founder Joe Mansueto believed that fundamental information should be widely available, and in 1984 created Morningstar to provide individual investors with much-needed mutual fund analysis and commentary.

In 1984, Morningstar published its first product, *The Mutual Fund Sourcebook*™, a quarterly publication containing performance data, portfolio holdings, and other information on approximately 400 mutual funds. In the 25-plus years since the *Sourcebook*'s first printing, Morningstar has served a key role in the investment community. Today Morningstar is one of the most recognized and trusted names in the investment industry and serves more than 8 million individual investors, 250,000 financial advisers, and 4,500 institutional clients around the world.

Morningstar has a strong reputation for independence and objectivity. It is also known for innovative contributions to the investment industry, particularly in bringing relevant information to a broad audience. Morningstar data and proprietary analytical tools include the Morningstar Rating™, which brings both performance and risk together into one evaluation, and the Morningstar Style Box™ which provides a visual summary of a fund's underlying investment style. Both have become important tools for millions of investors and advisers."

A typical rating screenshot is below and shows the Morningstar rating for a popular Vanguard fund. This fund received a Four-Star rating. Ratings range from one to five stars. The rating methodology is proprietary and is intended to include many relevant factors such as performance, fee structure, asset turnover and manager longevity, to name a few.

Morningstar ratings can be helpful tools in the evaluation of mutual funds to use from your 401K plan. However, a strong rating (based on historical performance) is no guarantee of future success. Remember, don't chase past historical returns, and remember the theory of reversion-to-the-mean.

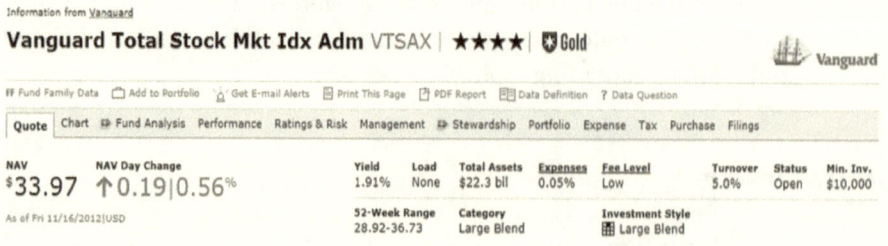

Chapter 4

Asset Allocation

Asset mix drives performance

"One should always divide his wealth into three parts: a third in land, a third in merchandise, and a third ready to hand."—*Babylonian Talmud: Tractate Baba Mezi'a*

The above quote comes from the Jewish Bible. It's amazing how true that quote remains even in today's modern world. Think about what that statement really means. One should divide one's wealth into three parts. One part in land, which is probably close to the portion of our own total assets represented by our primary residence; and/or investment property. The reference to one third in merchandise would equate to investments in today's world. These would represent a store of value that would likely go up over time and could be converted to cash if the situation required. And finally a third, ready to hand, means almost what it sounds like—cash or bonds. So in the end the Jewish Bible suggests an asset allocation of one-third liquid investments, one-third real estate, and finally one-third cash or bonds. While the real estate allocation in today's world may be a little high it's not far off. So in the end the Talmud's recommended asset allocation works even today. However, we will recommend some modifications from this ancient time-tested formula.

In this book we concentrate our asset allocation question around our 401K retirement assets. This would be the "merchandise" from the Talmud. Study after study has confirmed that long-term wealth is created through asset allocation much more so than individual stock selection (Ibbotson-Kaplan; Brinson, Hood and Beebower; Brinson, Beebower and Singer). In essence all the studies confirm that approximately 90% of a portfolio's long term variation in return is attributable to asset allocation, not individual stock selection. This is especially true in a 401K, where you don't have individual stock selection as an option. The typical pension fund will carry a 60/40 stock/bond asset allocation, or mix. Since pension funds have a long term investment horizon, just like us, we will use this 60/40 mix as a starting point.

If you're younger, say in your twenties or thirties, you would likely want a higher stock allocation. As you get into your forties and fifties the stock allocation would be reduced to the 60% level. As you get into your sixties and seventies the stock mix would be reduced even further, but given today's long life spans the equity mix should be maintained at some level. These baseline stock concentration levels could be further adjusted based upon your individual risk profile. For example, a twenty-five-year-old with an aggressive personality and investment style might have 80% to 85% of their investments in a diversified stock portfolio. Whereas, another twenty-five-year-old with a more conservative personality might only carry 65% to 70% stock mix, but the 60/40 split should always be viewed as the baseline.

In most plans, within the stock category there are many sub-sectors to choose from. Your plan will clearly denote which funds are stock funds.

The two primary categories are **growth** and **value**.

Growth companies are what their name suggests—companies with rapid growth. They may not have profitability yet, won't pay a dividend, and are usually newer businesses.

Value stocks are normally more mature companies, have slower growth, and often pay a high dividend.

There are many examples of companies that started out as growth companies and then matured into value companies. Some tech giants like Microsoft and Intel are good examples. In the 1980's and 1990's these companies defined what growth stocks looked like. They had rapid revenue growth, high earnings multiples, and did not pay dividends. Today, these mature companies meet more of the value criteria than the growth.

In addition, there are other sub-categories: large-cap, mid-cap, and small-cap. These categories are exactly what they sound like—large, medium and small sized companies as measured by their market capitalization (public value of their stock).

Some 401K plans will also offer some international stock funds, possibly emerging-market stock funds, and perhaps even some commodity funds that would invest in precious metals, natural resources, or even real estate.

The key to building a diversified common stock portfolio is to understand the correlations between the various fund classes. Correlation simply means how the various funds move together. Funds that are perfectly positively correlated move exactly the same way and in exactly the same degree. So if two funds are perfectly correlated and one goes up by 10% the other will go up by 10% as well. This also means that funds that are perfectly correlated go down together, too. If funds were negatively correlated then when one fund was up the other would be down and vice versa.

Finding funds that are negatively correlated to one another is like chasing the fountain of youth. The reason that negative correlation is so highly sought after is because of the buffering effect that negative correlation can have on the portfolio's performance. With such funds, when one part of the market goes down another part of the market would go up so that the net effect would be a slight increase. However, study after study has shown that in major market moves, especially downward ones, all asset classes tend to converge. This means that the old correlation rules go out the window and the gravity of a severe down-market takes everything with it. This was true in the 1991 recession, the 2001 recession, and most especially the 2008/ 2009 stock market collapse. So while the search for negatively correlated asset classes continues when it's needed most, i.e. a severe down-market, it simply doesn't hold. Nonetheless, it is only prudent to spread our stock investments across differing sectors.

On the bond side, we also have a host of investment choices. The first grouping would be commercial and government bonds. On the government side, there are long-term government bonds, long-term municipal bonds and global bonds. We have medium-term and short-term government bonds, and treasury inflation protected securities (TIPS).

On the commercial side, there are investment grade bonds, high-yield bonds, secured, unsecured, convertible bonds, and bonds that invest in bank loans and emerging market debt. The list of bond categories continues to grow. Again, your actual plan choices will vary based upon your employer's investment options. However, fixed income or bond asset classes will be clearly marked and easy to be recognized. Bonds are debt instruments—in essence, loans to a corporation, municipality or government.

Historically, long-term bonds have exhibited about half the level of risk of common stocks. Risk is defined for us as the standard deviation of returns around their mean, or average. High standard deviations mean more risk. The risky returns between stocks and bonds varies over time and can be quite wide or quite narrow depending upon the economic cycle at that time. According to the Institute of Business and Finance, during 2010 long-term US government bonds (20-year maturity) had a standard deviation of 13%, while large-cap US stocks (S&P 500) had a 22% standard deviation and medium-term US government bonds (five-year maturity) just 4%. This means long-term government bonds had 41% less risk than large stocks, while five-year government bonds had 82% less risk.

Most investors choose bond funds for their principal safety, the income generated, and as a diversification tool. If you hold the bond to maturity its principal balance is assured, assuming the issuer is still in business. However, if you needed to sell a bond prior to maturity its price could be quite different depending upon the interest rate environment at the time the bond is sold. According to the IBF, government bonds lost principal in six of the last fifteen years. The losses were higher for long-term bonds, as the table below shows.

20- year US Government Bond		5-year US government Bond	
Year of loss	Principal loss	Year of loss	Principal loss
1996	7.40%	1996	3.90%
1999	14.40%	1999	7.10%
2000	1.90%	2004	1.10%
2003	3.40%	2005	2.60%
2006	3.60%	2006	1.50%
2009	18.30%	2009	4.40%
average loss	8.20%	average loss	3.40%

From 1972 – 2010, the S&P 500 and five-year government bonds never suffered losses in the same calendar year (Institute for Business and Finance, 2011). If that's not enough motivation for you to diversify, nothing is.

Age and the asset allocation

"Youth is wasted on the young."—*George Bernard Shaw*

When it comes to investing, younger people have time on their side. However, they often squander this advantage because they choose to spend instead of save. A person with many years between today and retirement can absorb more of the ups and downs of the market than can someone within five or ten years of retirement. As a result, the younger you are, the higher the proportion of stocks you can have in your portfolio.

There is a simple convention used to determine the percentage of stocks for your age—the 100-point rule. This rule states that your stock allocation should be equal to 100 minus your age. For example, a 25-year old could hold up to 75% of their investment assets in stocks. The balance would be in bonds. Stocks have higher long-term returns than bonds, but along with the higher returns come more volatility (risk). Time can smooth out this volatility, which is why younger investors can afford more stocks than older investors. However, this overly simple guide ignores personal risk appetite and personal preference.

Pension funds would maintain a stock/bond mix of 60/40 as a baseline. On average, this asset mix would generate returns through market cycles that would enable to pension plan to have sufficient assets to pay its annual plan obligations. In years when the market was down substantially the plan assets might not be sufficient and additional contributions to the plan from the company may be required to maintain the plan's asset sufficiency.

I created an asset mix/risk profile matrix to help people maintain an appropriate mix of stocks and bonds in their 401K plans. The matrix below suggests a risk-adjusted mix of stocks and bonds for a given time horizon of years until retirement. The matrix assumes that retirement age is sixty-five, and ignores an annual asset mix re-balancing. This matrix can be used as a guideline to establish your personal asset mix given your risk appetite.

Risk Profile	Stock/Bond Asset Allocation				
Aggressive	90/10	80/20	70/30	60/40	50/50
Moderately Aggressive	80/20	70/30	60/40	50/50	40/60
Moderate	70/30	60/40	50/50	40/60	30/70
Moderately Conservative	60/40	50/50	40/60	30/70	20/80
Conservative	50/50	40/60	30/70	20/80	10/90
	30 - 40	20 - 30	10 - 20	6 - 10	5 - Retired
	Years until Retirement				

Using the matrix above, we can evaluate an asset mix for a twenty-five-year-old person with a moderate risk profile. For this person, they have forty years until retirement and could have a stock mix of 75% and bonds of 25%. This mix would adjust over time and after ten years when he/she has thirty years until retirement the asset mix could have shifted down to a 60/40 stock/bond mix. In the real world, changes in asset mix are not so linear. Changes in portfolio performance and re-balancing over time might make the asset mix deviate from "textbook" allocations over time. Again, this guideline allows for personal preference.

The table below shows the annual asset allocation glide-path over time for this example person.

Moderate			Moderate		
Age	Stock	Bond	Age	Stock	Bond
25	75	25	46	54	46
26	74	26	47	53	47
27	73	27	48	52	48
28	72	28	49	51	49
29	71	29	50	50	50
30	70	30	51	49	51
31	69	31	52	48	52
32	68	32	53	47	53
33	67	33	54	46	54
34	66	34	55	45	55
35	65	35	56	44	56
36	64	36	57	43	57
37	63	37	58	42	58
38	62	38	59	41	59
39	61	39	60	40	60
40	60	40	61	39	61
41	59	41	62	38	62
42	58	42	63	37	63
43	57	43	64	36	64
44	56	44	65	35	65
45	55	45			

Auto Enrollment

Many employers have started automatically enrolling new employees into the firm's 401K plan even if they do not opt in. Almost a quarter of large firms offer auto-enrollment to employees in 2012, up from 10% in 2009, according to a Towers Watson study. It is good that employees are being forced to save for their retirement however, those that are auto-enrolled often are not saving enough. This is because when employers auto-enroll an employee they often do so at a low contribution rate, typically about 3% of pay so they do not have to match as much. Employees can always change the default savings rate but too few do.

When asked what their contribution rate was, many workers had no idea what their contribution rate is/was. As I've said many times throughout this book, "You can't afford to ignore your 401K". When employees are auto-enrolled it is normally into a lifestyle fund. As we will discuss next, these are not always what they seem. So, if you do not know what your contribution rate is, go find out from your human resources contact person right away.

Lifestyle Funds

Mutual fund companies have created "lifestyle funds" designed to lessen the individual's involvement with annual portfolio re-balancing. These funds are calibrated with a mix of investments that reflect the investor's age group and presumed tolerance for risk. They also allow the fund manager the opportunity to vary stock/bond allocations to exploit his or her market expectations. For example, a fund manager believing that the market is historically undervalued might temporarily raise their stock or bond allocation in order to benefit from their market expectations. This can hurt the investors in such funds if the fund manager's expectations are not realized. The fund managers are not accountable to a single investor and fund managers change over time, so the effect of a fund manager's investing style can have a significant impact on fund value, good or bad.

Lifestyle funds also ignore the personal risk profile of the investor. Rather they assume all investors born in a calendar year have the same risk appetite and goals. Clearly, this is not the case. Take the Vanguard Target Retirement 2045 fund for example. According to the fund's investment strategy and objective, this fund "seeks to provide capital appreciation and current income consistent with its current asset allocation. The fund primarily invests in other Vanguard mutual funds according to an asset allocation strategy designed for investors planning to retire and leave the workforce in or within a few years of 2045 (the target year). Its asset allocation will become more conservative over time, meaning that the percentage of assets allocated to stocks will decrease while the percentage of assets allocated to bonds and other fixed income investments will increase."

As of the writing of this book (2012), this target date fund would have an investment horizon of about thirty-three years (2012 to 2045). This would equate to an individual approximately thirty-two years old. (Retire at sixty-five, minus the thirty-three-year time horizon nets an implied participant age of thirty-two.) On balance, you might expect the fund to be managed with a moderate risk appetite to compensate for the mix of individuals in the plan. If so, that would infer a stock/bond mix of approximately 70/30, meaning around 70% in stocks and 30% in bonds. However, the fund's asset mix at the time of this writing was:

Sector	% Assets
US Stocks	62.4%
Non-US Stocks	26.4%
Bonds	9.7%
Cash	0.9%
Other	0.6%
Total	100.0%

Note that the above stock/bond mix is 89/11—wow! That is a very aggressive stock/bond mix for individuals looking to retire in thirty-three years in the year 2045. There are no regulatory restrictions that limit the boundaries of the stock/bond mix that the target date fund manager chooses. This particular asset mix would likely underperform a more balanced portfolio when the markets decline because it would not benefit from the buffering effect of the bond portfolio's fixed income component. This asset mix might be very unsettling for a conservative investor, while suiting the aggressive investor just right.

Another problem with target date funds is the compounding (or layering in) effect of mutual fund fees. As this fund states, "the fund primarily invests in other Vanguard mutual funds." So even at a low cost fund family like The Vanguard Group, fees can get high in these target date funds. The 2045 target date fund had the following to ten holdings: Vanguard Total Stock Market Index Investor (VTSMX) 62.92%; Vanguard Total International Stock Index Investor (VGTSX), 26.89%; Vanguard Total Bond Market II Index Investor (VBMFX), 10.11%.

401K Tune-up: Do you really want to work 'til 80?

Fund	Exp ratio	% Holdings
VTSMX	0.18%	62.92%
VGTSX	0.22%	26.89%
VBMFX	0.22%	10.11%

This would equate to a weighted average expense ratio of 0.19%, and according to the Vanguard website the actual expense ratio is 0.19%, just as it should be.

However, when this fund was held in a TransAmerica-managed 401K account of one of my clients, the expense ratio was dramatically different. According to a TransAmerica report, "The Vanguard Target Retirement 2045 Ret Opt, a TLIC Separate Account, invests exclusively in the Vanguard Target Retirement 2045 Fund (Investor Class), a mutual fund (Fund)." The expense ratio of this TLIC separate account was a whopping 0.94%!

Investment Information

The Vanguard Target Retirement 2045 Ret Opt, a TLIC Separate Account, invests exclusively in the Vanguard Target Retirement 2045 Fund (Investor Class), a mutual fund (Fund).

Investment Objective & Strategy

The investment seeks to provide capital appreciation and current income consistent with its current asset allocation.

The fund primarily invests in other Vanguard mutual funds according to an asset allocation strategy designed for investors planning to retire and leave the work force in or within a few years of 2045 (the target year). Its asset allocation will become more conservative over time, meaning that the percentage of assets allocated to stocks will decrease while the percentage of assets allocated to bonds and other fixed income investments will increase.

Operations

Redemption Fee/Term	—
Expense Ratio	Type 7*: 0.94% of fund assets
Underlying Incept Date	10-27-03
Underlying Initial Share Class Incept Date	—
Separate Account Incept	10-05-04
Closed to New Investors	—
Trading Restrictions	—

*See Disclosure Page under "Charges, Fees and Expenses" for more details.

So this infers that TransAmerica Life Insurance Company (TLIC) is adding 0.75% to manage a fund of funds that is managed by other fund managers who charge significantly less than TransAmerica.

In footnote 7* they provide the definition of these fees.

Type 7: The expense ratio quoted reflects the maximum total operating expenses, of the investment choice, which include the Investment Management Charge and Administrative Charges assessed by Transamerica (if applicable), and the total operating expenses of the underlying investment, net of any fee waivers. There may also be charges to your balance in the separate accounts for contract asset charges, discontinuance charges or service fees, as applicable under your contract, which are not reflected on these factsheets.

What possible added value could TransAmerica provide to justify an additional 0.75%? The answer is, none!

However, you can clearly see the problems that arise with these fund-of-funds target date funds. While their concept may sound good, the actual portfolio mix may or may not align with your personal risk appetite, and fees can get compounded, which erode your retirement assets.

Portfolio Re-balancing

Portfolio rebalancing is one of the simplest things an investor can do to improve their long-term financial results, yet it is also the most ignored investor activity. As we discussed in the asset mix section, almost all of the portfolio's return comes from its asset allocation. Much time and energy is spent on determining the correct asset allocation for a given investor. However, almost no time is spent evaluating the asset allocation thereafter. Portfolio rebalancing is important for many reasons, most importantly because it resets the portfolio so that its risk level is in harmony with the client's.

Many studies have shown what happens to portfolios that are neglected or ignored. The results are fairly obvious. Over time the equity portion will grow to a disproportionate level and tilt the mix away from its original targeted allocation. If left unchecked a portfolio originally set to a 60/40 stock/bond mix can, over twenty years or so, easily turn into an 80/20 mix. The last thing an investor approaching retirement would want is a portfolio so inherently risky at the precise time when this investor is seeking retirement.

The key to rebalancing is to only do it about once a year. The benefits of rebalancing can be lost with rebalancing that occurs more frequently. So only look to rebalance one time per year.

Next, concentrate your rebalancing efforts on the stock/bond mix, and don't worry too much about the various subcategories within those two major categories of stocks and bonds. In the section of the book called Plan Review, we will go through a step-by-step approach on how to do an annual portfolio rebalancing. You will see that it's not very hard and only takes a few minutes to complete, but the return you get on this time investment will be substantial.

Chapter 5

Plan Administration

Max the match: How do you maximize the company match?

First, I should point out that your money is always yours, regardless of the company match. In addition, it does not matter how your employment with a company ends, you get terminated, or you quit. The money that you contribute to the plan is <u>always</u> yours.

The money your employer contributes, however, may be subject to a vesting schedule. Many companies have a 3-5 year vesting vesting schedule for the company match portion. It usually is an equal vesting each year. For example, a three-year vesting would be 1/3 each year for three years. So, if you are planning to leave and are near a vesting point, you may want to re-think your departure date.

Here are two examples of common matching schemes offered by employers.

1. Fifty percent match up to the first six percent. In this plan, the employer will contribute $0.50 into your 401K plan for every $1.00 you do. In this plan the employer's match is capped at 6% of your gross salary, and their match will be 3% (50% of the 6% cap). The table below shows an example of this plan and its associated economics. You can see that someone who contributes nothing gets nothing. Also, if you contribute the maximum ($17,500 in the example), your match is not 50%, rather it is only 8.57%. This is still a guaranteed return, and noting to be ashamed of, but most people think the 50% match is all the way up the contribution levels. It is not.

		6%	3%		Actual Match %	Total	Contribution %
Salary	Max Contribution	Conbtribution	Co Match	Match %	Contribution	Contribution	Salary
$ 30,000	$ 17,500	NONE MADE	$ -		0.00% $	-	0.00%
$ 30,000	$ 17,500	$ 1,800	$ 900	50.00%	5.14% $	18,400	61.33%
$ 35,000	$ 17,500	$ 2,100	$ 1,050	50.00%	6.00% $	18,550	53.00%
$ 40,000	$ 17,500	$ 2,400	$ 1,200	50.00%	6.86% $	18,700	46.75%
$ 45,000	$ 17,500	$ 2,700	$ 1,350	50.00%	7.71% $	18,850	41.89%
$ 50,000	$ 17,500	$ 3,000	$ 1,500	50.00%	8.57% $	19,000	38.00%
$ 60,000	$ 17,500	$ 3,600	$ 1,800	50.00%	10.29% $	19,300	32.17%
$ 70,000	$ 17,500	$ 4,200	$ 2,100	50.00%	12.00% $	19,600	28.00%
$ 80,000	$ 17,500	$ 4,800	$ 2,400	50.00%	13.71% $	19,900	24.88%
$ 90,000	$ 17,500	$ 5,400	$ 2,700	50.00%	15.43% $	20,200	22.44%
$100,000	$ 17,500	$ 6,000	$ 3,000	50.00%	17.14% $	20,500	20.50%
$110,000	$ 17,500	$ 6,600	$ 3,300	50.00%	18.86% $	20,800	18.91%
$120,000	$ 17,500	$ 7,200	$ 3,600	50.00%	20.57% $	21,100	17.58%
$130,000	$ 17,500	$ 7,800	$ 3,900	50.00%	22.29% $	21,400	16.46%
$140,000	$ 17,500	$ 8,400	$ 4,200	50.00%	24.00% $	21,700	15.50%
$150,000	$ 17,500	$ 9,000	$ 4,500	50.00%	25.71% $	22,000	14.67%
$160,000	$ 17,500	$ 9,600	$ 4,800	50.00%	27.43% $	22,300	13.94%
$170,000	$ 17,500	$ 10,200	$ 5,100	50.00%	29.14% $	22,600	13.29%
$180,000	$ 17,500	$ 10,800	$ 5,400	50.00%	30.86% $	22,900	12.72%
$190,000	$ 17,500	$ 11,400	$ 5,700	50.00%	32.57% $	23,200	12.21%
$200,000	$ 17,500	$ 12,000	$ 6,000	50.00%	34.29% $	23,500	11.75%
$210,000	$ 17,500	$ 12,600	$ 6,300	50.00%	36.00% $	23,800	11.33%
$220,000	$ 17,500	$ 13,200	$ 6,600	50.00%	37.71% $	24,100	10.95%
$230,000	$ 17,500	$ 13,800	$ 6,900	50.00%	39.43% $	24,400	10.61%
$240,000	$ 17,500	$ 14,400	$ 7,200	50.00%	41.14% $	24,700	10.29%
$250,000	$ 17,500	$ 15,000	$ 7,500	50.00%	42.86% $	25,000	10.00%
$260,000	$ 17,500	$ 15,600	$ 7,800	50.00%	44.57% $	25,300	9.73%
$270,000	$ 17,500	$ 16,200	$ 8,100	50.00%	46.29% $	25,600	9.48%
$280,000	$ 17,500	$ 16,800	$ 8,400	50.00%	48.00% $	25,900	9.25%
$290,000	$ 17,500	$ 17,400	$ 8,700	50.00%	49.71% $	26,200	9.03%
$300,000	$ 17,500	$ 17,500	$ 8,750	50.00%	50.00% $	26,250	8.75%
$310,000	$ 17,500	$ 17,500	$ 8,750	50.00%	50.00% $	26,250	8.47%

SAMPLE VESTING SCHEDULE OF A BASIC 6% CONTRIBUTION, 3% COMPANY MATCH PLAN

2. Dollar for dollar match up to five percent. Here, for every $1.00 you contribute the employer will add $1.00 up to a limit of 5% of your gross salary. Once your contributions hit 5% the employer stops matching for that year.

Commissions and bonuses

If your compensation includes commissions or bonuses you have to be especially careful how your contributions are made if you want to "max the match." For example, suppose you had a base salary of $50,000 and got an annual bonus of $10,000 paid in January of the following year. You decide that since the bonus is a windfall, you'll fund your annual 6% 401K contribution out of that and then have the benefit of a higher paycheck throughout the year since your 6% match is fully funded. (I assume in this example the contribution of the employee is desired to be six percent.) So, the payroll department deducts $3,000 from your bonus and puts it in the 401K. Since you funded the entire contribution at once, some plans will only fund a part of this $3,000, since "at the time" the cumulative contribution divided by the cumulative compensation is less than six percent. Therefore, you would only receive a company match of

Annual salary:	$50,000
Pay periods in a year:	26
Cumulative Compensation as of January 31st.	$13,846.15 ($10,000 bonus + 1/13 of annual salary)
401K contribution Amount:	$3,000
Contribution percentage:	21.66% (3,000/$13,846.15)
Result:	You hit the 6% company match
Effect:	$415.38 company match for the year!

The company matched 3% of your compensation up to your contribution of 6%. Since you hit the 6% in the first month, they match the 3% of your year-to-date compensation, not 50% of your contribution. So, 3% of your year-to-date salary of $13,846.15 is only $415.38.

Make sure if you have any variable compensation you do not have 401K contributions deducted. Instead, have your 401K contributions set to equal your annual contribution amount divided by the number of pay periods in a year. That way, you will hit your annual target in the final pay period and get the full match.

If your 401K contribution was not matched the way you expected it to get matched, contact your human resources department and speak to the 401K plan administrator to learn why. Then do what you need to in order to max the match the following year. This part of the plan, the company match, can be very tricky. You do not want to find out ten years into a plan that you missed out on company-matched funds. Don't ignore this. It's too important, and as you know by now: "You can't afford to ignore it!"

So how do you get the maximum match? This is a 50% match on your maximum contribution amount of $17,500?

It's easy, but hard.

First take your desired contribution amount, in this case the legal limit of $17,500.

Next divide that by the maximum company match. In this example they match 50% of the first 6%, so divide by six percent. The result is $291,666.67!

If your base salary equals (or exceeds) this amount you could get matched contributions equal to ½ of the federal contribution maximum. In this case the match would be $8,750, or exactly 50% of the maximum federally permitted tax-deductible 401K contribution amounts (for this example year).

So if you really want to "max the match" you better get a raise! However, isn't it interesting that the only people who actually get the maximum company match are probably the same people who approved the company plan?

This is no coincidence, is it?

Family Planning

Another client is a young couple with a new baby. Two college educated professionals who are both aware of their need to save for their retirement. The husband works for Verizon and the wife for a local manufacturer. They came to me asking about ways they could save intelligently and maximize the value of their savings. I studied each of their employer plans and found an interesting thing—the match in the Verizon plan was $1.00 for $1.00, up to 6%. His wife's plan was a more traditional 50% of the first 6% saved matching.

They were not able to afford to save the 6% maximum match levels at both employers. They have a young baby and family expenses limit what they can reasonably afford to save. Given the terrific matching at Verizon, I suggested they concentrate their family savings in the Verizon account where they can get the maximum match. Then whatever else they can afford to save would be in the spouse's plan at the manufacturer.

This situation is not uncommon. When married couples evaluate their savings plan, they need to keep in mind the attributes of each employer's plan and fund the most generous one to its limit. Then fund the remainder at the other plan.

Your beneficiary

When was the last time you updated your plan beneficiary? Yes, that's right, it's been so long you don't even remember setting one. So, the next day you go to work, call the human resources person and ask for a beneficiary change form. Fill it out and send it back. You don't want your ex-spouse to get the money, do you?

You think to yourself, "But I have a will so I'm covered, right?"

Not so, because plan rules govern what happens to the assets upon your death. The plan will not consider a will's instructions.

As we go through life, events may occur which could impact your retirement savings. For instance, a marriage or a divorce will clearly impact who you would want to receive your retirement plan account balance in the event of your untimely death. Therefore, it is important that you periodically review your beneficiary selection.

Please take the time to make sure that you have designated a beneficiary for any benefits that would become payable upon your death. At the same time, you should also make sure that the beneficiary you have selected meets your estate planning objectives. If you fail to designate a beneficiary, the terms of your plan will determine your beneficiary and that could trigger estate taxes you need not pay. In the absence of a beneficiary designation, a plan will typically deem the spouse to be the beneficiary for a married participant and the estate for an unmarried participant.

It should be noted that in order to designate a beneficiary you must complete the plan's beneficiary designation form. The plan will not recognize any beneficiaries that you may designate in your will or any other forms related to your estate.

Update your beneficiary!

Hardship Withdrawals

There are several ways to take money out of a 401K plan but many of them result in early withdrawal penalties and the money taken treated as taxable income. As a result, you really shouldn't take money out of your 401K plan unless it's a dire emergency. According to the IRS, A retirement plan may, but is not required to, provide for hardship distributions. Many plans that provide for elective deferrals provide for hardship distributions. Thus, 401K plans, 403B plans, and 457B plans may permit hardship distributions.

If a 401K plan provides for hardship distributions, it must provide the specific criteria used to make the determination of hardship. Thus, for example, a plan may provide that a distribution can be made only for medical or funeral expenses, but not for the purchase of a principal residence or for payment of tuition and education expenses. In determining the existence of a need and of the amount necessary to meet the need, the plan must specify and apply nondiscriminatory and objective standards.

For a distribution from a 401K plan to be on account of hardship, it must be made on account of an immediate and heavy financial need of the employee and the amount must be necessary to satisfy the financial need. The need of the employee includes the need of the employee's spouse or dependent. (Reg. §1.401K-1(d)(3)(i))

Under the provisions of the Pension Protection Act of 2006, the need of the employee also may include the need of the employee's non-spouse, non-dependent beneficiary.

Whether a need is immediate and heavy depends on the facts and circumstances. Certain expenses are deemed to be immediate and heavy, including: (1) certain medical expenses; (2) costs relating to the purchase of a principal residence; (3) tuition and related educational fees and expenses; (4) payments necessary to prevent eviction from, or foreclosure on, a principal residence; (5) burial or funeral expenses; and (6) certain expenses for the repair of damage to the employee's principal residence. A financial need may be immediate and heavy even if it was reasonably foreseeable or voluntarily incurred by the employee. The key question with any hardship withdrawal is what your employer's plan will allow.

Start-Up Capital

In the wake of the 2009/2010 great recession and skyrocketing unemployment rates, some laid-off employees have decided to start their own businesses and tap their 401K plan for their startup capital. In general, I would say that taking money out of your 401K plan for any purpose other than your retirement is extremely dangerous. However, sometimes people find themselves in dire straits and have no other choice but to raid their 401K plans. As some people sought a level of self-control over their employment prospects they started their own businesses. Most people are aware of the exceedingly high failure rate of startup businesses. However, many startups succeed and can provide stable income for their owners for many years to come.

I have seen several franchise businesses that work with 401K conversion companies. These companies people help convert their 401K plan to an ERISA profit-sharing plan. These are called Rollovers as Business Start-ups, or (ROBS). Next, the profit-sharing plan invests in shares of the newly formed company. This tactic avoids any early withdrawal penalties and it is legal but risky in that if your business fails, you could be totally wiped out.

In 2009 alone, 4,050 businesses—60 percent of them franchises—were launched with retirement rollover money, according to FRANdata, an independent research firm. These new entrepreneurs started ventures that range from data processing companies to flower shops, created more than 60,000 new jobs and added $8.3 billion to the nation's economy. And the lingering recession, says Steve Rosen, CEO of FranNet, a franchise broker firm based in Louisville, Ky., is only making retirement rollovers more attractive.

According to a July 2010 Entrepreneur Magazine article, "The practice began in earnest in 2000, when industry founders and former business associates Leonard Fischer, now CEO of BeneTrends Inc., and Steven Cooper, now CEO of SDCooper Co., pioneered this concept for franchisors.

The three main administrators of rollover plans—SDCooper, BeneTrends and Guidant Financial Group Inc.—have tweaked ERISA rules into a neat three-step program. According to their websites, you pay one of them a fee of about $5,000 and they'll do the rest: Move your current 401K or IRA (self-directed IRAs are not eligible) into an ERISA profit-sharing plan, which then becomes the retirement plan for your new company." That plan buys up the stock of your new C-corporation. Once the funds have transferred, they become tax-free capital for your business. In essence, you are spending the money on your own corporation instead of for stock of another company, such as General Electric or Goldman Sachs.

While I don't endorse using your 401K plan assets as startup capital for a new business I recognize that many people have no choice and have no other place to go for startup capital. If you are one of these people at least be careful and only invest as little as possible of your 401K plan assets in your new business. By no means should you invest more than 50% of your plan assets into this new business. Investing more than 50% is simply just too risky.

According to the IRS' ROBS Project, results indicate that, "Although there were some success stories, most ROBS businesses either failed or were on the road to failure with high rates of bankruptcy (business and personal), liens (business and personal), and corporate dissolutions by individual Secretaries of State. Some of the individuals who started ROBS plans lost not only the retirement assets they accumulated over many years, but also their dream of owning a business. As a result, much of the retirement savings invested in their unsuccessful ROBS plan was depleted or 'lost,' in many cases even before they had begun to offer their product or service to the public."

So again, be careful with how you use your 401K plan assets, a lot is at stake.

401K Loans

Another way to legally remove funds from your 401K plan without incurring early withdrawal penalties or adverse tax effects is by taking a 401K loan. However, not all plans offer this feature. If offered, the amount you can borrow is generally limited to the lesser of 50% of the vested balance of your plan assets, or $50,000. The early withdrawal penalties do not apply unless you leave your employer and are unable to pay back the loan balance at that time.

If you borrow from your plan, the loan payments are deducted from your pay after tax and when you do withdraw the money at retirement it will be taxed again. The employer determines the loan terms and interest rates charged. However, most employers offer loan terms up to 5 years with interest rates fixed at the prime rate plus a margin, anywhere from 0% to 2%. Any interest you pay on the loan is paid back to your account as if it were a fixed income bond.

Borrowing against your 401K plan balance should really be a last resort. In order to get the funds for your loan some of your investments will have to be sold. The interest rate on your loan could be substantially below the overall investment performance of your plan assets. This would result in your retirement assets being below the amount needed for your retirement. While borrowing against 401K plan assets is not advised, I understand that in the real world it is sometimes necessary. Just be sure you understand the risks involved and pay back the loan as quickly as possible.

Chapter 6

Plan Review

Okay, we've covered the history of retirement plans, dissected a mutual fund, learned about the importance of asset allocation, and also learned about plan administration and associated costs.

Now it's time to do a plan review and select the appropriate funds for a recent client review. He's a thirty-five-year-old male, married with two children, and his spouse is a homemaker. Of course, our candidate could just as easily be a female with a spouse and children.

The first thing were going to do is go to his plan's information set, which could be on the Internet or available through your human resources representative. What we want is a list of available investment options and if possible associated performance and fees.

The plan that we are going to analyze is a plan administered by John Hancock pension services. This particular plan is from a financial institution, unaffiliated with John Hancock. So given that this particular employer is itself a financial institution I would hope that the plan would be better than the average. As you will see—there are an abundance of investment options to choose from, which could make things even more difficult for the average employee. Sometimes too many choices is as bad as not enough.

This particular plan offers exactly eighty different investment options. That is a huge number of choices. If all of the employees were sophisticated financial professionals then maybe that would be fine, but that's not the case. When faced with such a huge number of choices I would not be surprised to find many participants not just confused but bewildered.

The John Hancock website is very helpful and provides a lot of useful information. So that's a good place to start.

One of the views on their website for this particular customer allowed you to group the investment options by investment category as assigned by Morningstar, the mutual fund rating agency. Let me review with you the listing of the various investment categories and number of funds within each category.

Mutual Fund Type	2011	2012
Large-cap value	5	5
Large-cap blend	2	2
Large-cap growth	4	4
Mid-cap value	3	3
Mid-cap growth	4	4
Small-cap value	3	3
Small-cap blend	1	1
Small-cap growth	2	2
Multi-cap blend	2	2
International/ global value	5	5
International/ global blend	3	2
International/ global growth	3	4
Balanced fund	3	3
Index funds	6	6
Sector funds	7	7
High-quality short term fixed income	2	1
High-quality intermediate term fixed income	2	2
High-quality long-term fixed income	1	1
Medium quality intermediate term fixed income	2	2
High-yield bond	1	1
Global bond	1	1
Three-year guaranteed account	2	0
Five-year guaranteed account	2	0
Ten-year guarantee account	2	0
Asset allocation lifecycle	14	14
Total fund choices	80	75

Now that's a lot of funds to analyze! The other thing you see is that plans change year-to-year. Some fund selections are removed and others added.

That is why the annual rebalance is so important. However, when we break the funds back into the investment category choices we can shrink the number of categories within which we will need to review individual mutual funds. Some fund categories will be ignored altogether for this particular candidate. For example, this particular candidate did not want any of the guaranteed accounts, nor did he wish to consider any of the asset allocation lifecycle accounts. So right off the bat, we cut the choices by twenty. Nonetheless, sixty fund choices is still a lot of choice.

Personal investment profile

In this analysis we are focused solely on the 401K retirement plan. We are not looking at other financial planning aspects of this particular candidate at this time. The goal is to establish appropriate investment categories and fund choices for this person given the plan provided by his employer. This candidate is a moderately sophisticated finance person. That just means this person has worked in a financial services industry and has a finance or accounting background.

In my preliminary discussions with the candidate I thought he was a confident aggressive investor. However, the results of his investor risk profile showed that was not the case. The candidate found the assessment results mildly amusing since he too characterized himself as an aggressive investor. The real key to the temperance of his aggressive style was his family situation and age. No longer in his twenties, single, with no children, this man is the sole breadwinner for his household. He simply cannot afford to take the degree of risk he did even ten years ago. When we sat down and discussed the family situation and retirement timeline he saw this to be true and adopted a more conservative but still slightly aggressive investment posture.

That's the first part of the process determining your investor risk profile. You can obtain a copy of the risk assessment from my website, www.401kTune-Up.com.

The second step in the process is determining the appropriate asset allocation between stocks and bonds. We started with our base asset allocation of 60/40, meaning 60% of the investments would be in equity categories and the remaining 40% would be in bonds. Given his risk personality tempered by his lifestyle reality he chose to adopt a 65/35 split. As we get into the composition of the equity/bond mix we can talk further about additional risk and appropriate funds selection. We will start with the equity category.

We know that asset allocation is what drives investor return. Equities have the highest return but also the highest risk as measured by the volatility of returns over time. Over long periods of time this volatility is tempered.

However, one does not always know when volatility temperance is at its lowest or its highest. If you have a retirement portfolio highly concentrated in equities and were planning to retire in 2008, the market rocked your world. Chances are, that person was unable to retire and is still working today. The whole point of this book and our methodology is to best prepare you for your retirement regardless of market conditions when you choose to retire. That's a big goal but if we follow the plan it's a goal that is achievable. Now we will go back to the equity choices from our plan and see which ones this candidate believes are most suitable for him and his family.

Fund selection

After establishing a 65/35 stock bond mix the next step is to determine how each category will be invested.

We'll start with the equity components that will add up to 65% of the total. Within the equity category the first decision is how much international exposure does the candidate wish. This particular candidate believes that much of the growth in the global stock market will come from outside the US over his thirty-year remaining work horizon. Remember, this candidate is thirty-five years old and plans to retire in thirty years at age sixty-five.

Given his view, he decided to allocate 20% of his total to international equities. That will leave 45% of his total for domestic equities. Within the domestic equities he chose to go with a large cap blend for 15%, small-cap growth for 10%, small-cap value for 5%, sector category of 5% and finally he chose to put the balance of 10% into an S&P 500 index fund.

His decision for this fund mix was based on his belief that the large-cap category would behave much like a steady index fund especially given his choice for the large-cap blend as opposed to the value or growth. As we discussed in the asset allocation chapter, there is much debate and ample evidence suggesting that value stocks outperform growth stocks over long periods of time. Another effect that we saw was the performance of small cap stocks over large-cap stocks.

Given this, the candidate decided to split his equities mostly between large and small cap funds, skipping over the mid cap funds altogether.

Hedging his bet on the value versus growth debate, he decided to opt to split his small-cap position between growth and value.

Next, he believed that with the aging population of baby boomers and overweighting in the healthcare sector would be a good choice so he elected to allocate 5% to that sector. I pointed out that perhaps a better sector choice might be real estate. A little real estate exposure might help to buffer the stock bond behavior of his portfolio over his investment horizon. However, he did not want to absorb any real estate exposure in his retirement plan as he believes he's getting real estate exposure through his primary residence.

Other choices in the sector category included science and technology, energy, financial services, and utilities. Given that this portfolio review took place in 2011 when gold and commodities were skyrocketing in value, I was surprised that with its eighty fund choices there was not a commodity choice among the sectors. Nonetheless, we can only choose from what is presented.

Lastly, again to provide some stability in his equity performance when compared to the Standard & Poor's 500 index, he put 10% of his equity investments into an index fund.

After establishing the equity subcategories, we can move on to bond category selections. Although this 401K plan offered over fifty equity choices it offered only nine bond choices. The bond choices are subcategorized as follows:

High-quality short term fixed income	2
High-quality intermediate term fixed income	2
High-quality long-term fixed income	1
Medium quality intermediate term fixed income	2
High-yield bond	1
Global bond	1
Total bond funds	9

Again, this portfolio review took place in 2011, when interest rates were at record lows. With our candidate having a thirty-year investment horizon, he did not believe that any long-term fixed income funds would be a good fit for him. That is because (as we discussed in the asset allocation chapter) when interest rates rise, bond values fall. The longer the remaining maturity of a bond the more interest-rate sensitive it is. So even though the interest rates were higher on long-term fixed income portfolios, his belief was that these portfolios would not hold their value if inflation and interest rates rose. This is sound reasoning and I did not disagree. Nonetheless, he does need to have some fixed income exposure.

We had a discussion about high quality versus medium quality versus junk-bond quality bond funds. The reader may recall high-yield bonds used to be called junk bonds. That term has been mostly substituted with the label "high yield" instead. Regardless of what you call it, these are high-rate, high-risk bonds. Since their creation by Michael Milken in the 1980s, there has been a substantial amount of research done on the performance of high-yield bond funds. Many studies suggest that high-yield bond funds perform more like equities than bonds. So when looking at a total asset allocation one might consider a portion of the high-yield bond fund as additional pseudo-equity exposure. I only point that out so that people don't go too heavy into the high-yield bond fund because of its relatively attractive yield. Remember, there are no free lunches, and with high return comes high risk.

In the end, the candidate decided to put 15% of his funds in the medium-quality intermediate-term fixed income category. He felt this gave him a good balance between time horizon (intermediate term) and risk profile (medium quality). It was a sound selection.

Next, continuing with his view of global growth he wanted to put 10% of his portfolio in global bond fund. Given there's only one choice in this category that will be an easy selection.

Lastly, he wanted to have 10% of his portfolio in the high-yield bond fund. This too, will be an easy selection as there is only one high-yield bond fund to choose from.

So with that, the asset allocation categories are complete for our 65/35 stock bond mix. Next up is to review which individual funds under these categories should be selected. To summarize, the candidate's category investment allocation is as follows:

International Stocks	20%
Domestic Stocks	
Large Cap Blend	15%
Small Cap Growth	10%
Small Cap Value	5%
Sector—Healthcare	5%
S&P 500 Index	10%
Total Equity	65%

Medium Quality, Intermediate Term Bond Fund	15%
Global Bond	10%
High Yield	10%
Total Bond	35%

I should caution the reader at this point. Remember the reason you are reading this book and studying this material is so that you can create the best possible investment outcome for your 401K. Do not copy the asset allocation above, falsely believing that it is a recommended investment allocation for you. It is not. I know some people look for shortcuts and may simply feel overwhelmed and attempt to copy the allocations above. Please don't do that. You've gotten this far in the book; stick with it. I present this example only in an attempt to show you how the process actually works and its iterative nature. Once we sit down and go through the various fund choices within the categories we may find some funds are just simply unacceptable. If so, we may have to go back and adjust our allocations to reflect that unacceptability. Remember, this is not just about getting the asset allocation to match your personal profile it's also about picking the best funds.

We'll take each category one at a time and attempt to fill out our actual fund selections in the context of the desired category allocations. So let's begin by looking at the international stock funds available to this candidate. Within the international category we have several fund subcategories from which to choose.

International global value
International global blend
International global growth
International balanced funds
International stock index funds

Again, we see the separation of growth stocks and value stocks within this category. Remember growth versus value is an important distinction for equity investing.

This particular plan offers three international index funds to choose from. There is the John Hancock international growth, American funds euro pacific growth fund, and Franklin Templeton's mutual global discovery fund. The candidate wants his international stock exposure to be indexed. So, we will select from among these three funds.

The John Hancock international growth fund is described as a foreign large-cap stock blend as is the American Funds' Euro Pacific growth fund. The difference is that the American Funds focus on European and Pacific Rim stocks. The Franklin Templeton funds are described as a world stock fund.

As before, we start with the Finra fund analysis tool and section I, the fund summary.

	John Hancock International Growth Fund Class I	American Funds EuroPacific Growth Fund Class R5	Mutual Global Discovery Fund Class Z
Data as of:	11/12/2012	11/12/2012	11/23/2012
Ticker Symbol	GOIOX	RERFX	MDISX
Investment Amount $	10,000 $	10,000 $	10,000
Estimated Return you selected	8.00%	8.00%	8.00%
Holding Period Years	20	20	20
Fund Value after 10 Years $	37,033.63 $	41,754.89 $	38,085.15
Profit/(Loss) $	27,033.63 $	31,754.89 $	28,085.15
Total Fees and Sales Charges $	4,749.19 $	2,444.02 $	4,242.53
Total Fees $	4,749.19 $	2,444.02 $	4,242.53
Total Sales Charges $	- $	- $	-

Right away we see the maxim fund balance would be in the American Fund. It also has the lowest cumulative fee. That alone, however is not enough to decide on it. We need more information first.

Next we look carefully at the expense section.

	John Hancock International Growth Fund Class I	American Funds EuroPacific Growth Fund Class R5	Mutual Global Discovery Fund Class Z
Annual Operating Expenses	1.15%	0.55%	1.01%
Prospecttive Objective	Fees > Average of similar Foreign Stock Funds: 1.12%	Fees < Average of similar Foreign Stock Funds: 1.40%	Fees < Average of similar World Stock Funds: 1.10%
Morningstar Category	Fees < Average of similar Foreign Large Growth Funds: 1.28%	Fees < Average of similar Foreign Large Blend Funds: 1.33%	Fees < Average of similar World Stock Funds: 1.14%
Morningstar Rating (3 year)	Fees > Average of similar Morningstar Rated Funds: 0.86%	Fees < Average of similar Morningstar Rated Funds: 1.16%	Fees > Average of similar Morningstar Rated Funds: 0.78%

Again, we see the rewards of low expense rations. The American Funds expense ratio is the lowest of the three and appears well below its category peers. It is a curious note to see the different fund expense ratios as reported in the 401K plan report and then as compared to the Finra analysis. The table below explains.

Fund	Ticker	John Hancock 401K Plan Expense Ratio	Finra Expense Ratio
JH International Growth	GOIOX	1.15%	1.15%
American Funds	RERFX	1.00%	0.55%
Franklin Templeton	MDISX	1.26%	1.01%

The difference in fees charged in the John Hancock administered 401K Plan represent additional plan administration fees above and beyond the inherent fund fees charged by the actual fund itself. This still makes the American Fund our best choice, but the margin is slimmer. Further, the John Hancock fund which has no additional fund fees beyond the fund itself comes in second, instead of third. This is a good example of fee-layering that we discussed when reviewing Lifestyle funds. You may recall Lifestyle funds are often just funds of funds managed to monitor the stock/bond mix for a set period of time.

Lastly, we see the fund style box from Finra.

Fund Details			
	John Hancock International Growth Fund Class I	American Funds EuroPacific Growth Fund Class R5	Mutual Global Discovery Fund Class Z
Investment Objective	Foreign Stock	Foreign Stock	World Stock
Ticker Symbol	GOIOX	RERFX	MDISX
Minimum Initial Purchase	$ -	$ -	$ 1,000.00
Average Annual Return 1 Year	11.20%	7.78%	12.15%
Average Annual Return 5 Year	-3.01%	-3.07%	0.87%
Average Annual Return 10 Year	na	9.97%	10.43%
Average Annual Return Lifetime	3.52%	7.53%	12.09%
Morningstar Rating 3-Year (Stars)	Four	Four	Four

The Fund details box just helps us cement our selection. We see the funds all have 4-star Morningstar ratings, so that doesn't help distinguish one fund from another. All three are large capital funds but while two are growth oriented the Franklin Templeton fund is a value fund. We can also see the average returns for each fund and if there are any additional fees or charges. So based on the overall better net fund performance and low fees this client went with the American Funds Euro Pacific Fund for his international exposure.

The same approach would be taken for each other category where there is more than one choice. Us the Finra web tool to determine which fund in a particular fund category you will choose.

Plan 2—young, single mom

Another example is that of a young client who is just starting out. Her employer auto-enrolled her in their savings plan and placed her in a Lifestyle fund. That was the good news at least she had started saving. However, as we have seen the lifestyle funds are not always the best investment choice.

The first thing we did was asses her risk profile and then compared that to the risk profile of her investments. This comparison is shown in the chart below.

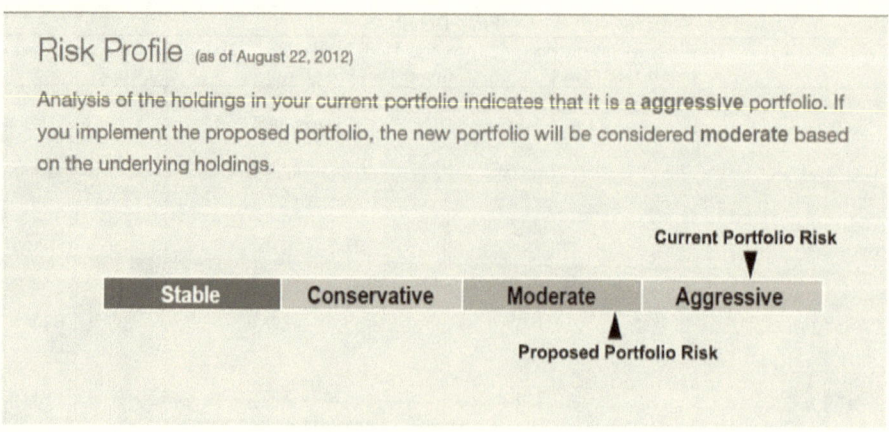

The analysis showed that her portfolio was aggressively positioned and that was not in line with her personality. So the first thing we did was to lower the risk profile of her investments.

A comparison of her beginning portfolio and the simple adjustments we made is below:

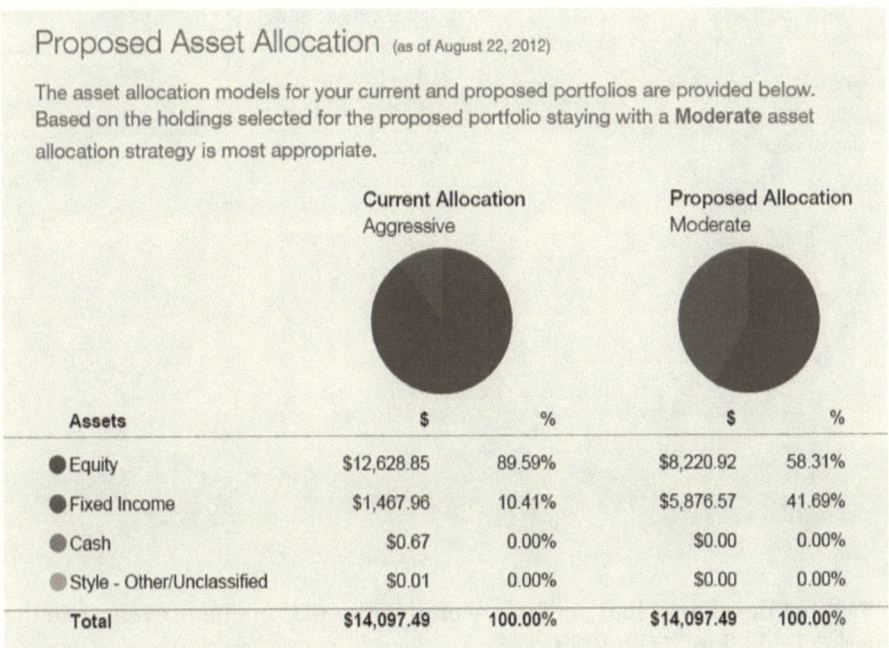

Proposed Asset Allocation (as of August 22, 2012)

The asset allocation models for your current and proposed portfolios are provided below. Based on the holdings selected for the proposed portfolio staying with a **Moderate** asset allocation strategy is most appropriate.

Assets	Current Allocation Aggressive		Proposed Allocation Moderate	
	$	%	$	%
● Equity	$12,628.85	89.59%	$8,220.92	58.31%
● Fixed Income	$1,467.96	10.41%	$5,876.57	41.69%
● Cash	$0.67	0.00%	$0.00	0.00%
● Style - Other/Unclassified	$0.01	0.00%	$0.00	0.00%
Total	$14,097.49	100.00%	$14,097.49	100.00%

Her portfolio was roughly 90/10 split between equities and fixed income (bonds). By adjusting the mix toward bonds we were able to buffer her investments against downturns but still give her the long-term growth she would need. In her case, we used a high yield bond fund because that has characteristics of both fixed income and equity. This was a better fixed income vehicle for her especially given her age.

The results of the re-balancing show the improvement in performance over the time period tested.

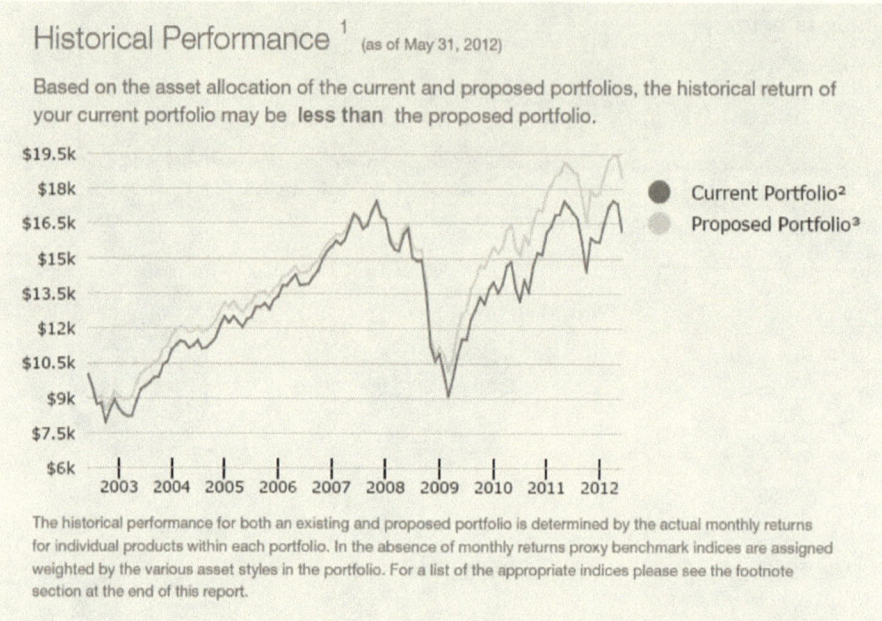

Historical Performance [1] (as of May 31, 2012)

Based on the asset allocation of the current and proposed portfolios, the historical return of your current portfolio may be **less than** the proposed portfolio.

● Current Portfolio[2]
● Proposed Portfolio[3]

The historical performance for both an existing and proposed portfolio is determined by the actual monthly returns for individual products within each portfolio. In the absence of monthly returns proxy benchmark indices are assigned weighted by the various asset styles in the portfolio. For a list of the appropriate indices please see the footnote section at the end of this report.

What the above chart shows is overall better performance, even when the market tanked in 2008/2009.

Annual rebalance

In an earlier chapter, I discussed the great importance of annual portfolio rebalancing. In this section, we'll actually go through a portfolio rebalancing exercise. We'll start by listing the mutual funds in our 401K plan by major category—stock or bond. Then within each category we list the various mutual funds and their associated dollar value. In the column next to the dollar value we calculate the percentage allocation of each fund and the summation for each fund category. All you need to do is take the dollar value of each fund and divide that by the total dollar value of your 401K. In the example below we see that the investor had a stock/bond mix of 65/35 at the end of last year. Now, one year later the investor is comparing the results.

The next set of columns is called the current year's values. Here we're simply adding the relative value of each of the funds at the rebalance date. We calculate the same relative percentages of the total 401K plan value and then compare these results with our target. To the extent that our asset allocation is less than desired we'll need to buy more of that fund. Conversely, if we find that our asset allocation is more than desired we will need to sell some of those funds in order to regain our target allocations.

This can be seen in the columns titled "Actions to Take." Here we're selling four funds and using the proceeds to buy more of another fund. Once these transactions are complete we verify that our new allocations are back in line with our target allocations.

It really is that simple of an exercise. Once you do it you'll see how simple and easy it is to do. You can also take satisfaction in knowing that you've gone a long way toward protecting your retirement assets. After you do this exercise a few years it will take you almost no time to complete the exercise and you get into a comfortable routine. You'll be able to rebalance your portfolio in less time than it takes to have the oil changed on your car. Approximately ten minutes is all it will take.

Plan Investment Choices	Last Year's Values		Current Year's Values		Actions to Take		Rebalanced Portfolio	
	Value	Target Allocation %	Value	Actual Allocation %			Value	Actual Allocation %
Bonds (35%):	$ 68,804	35.00%	$ 70,937	35.92%			$ 69,119	35.00%
Bond Index Fund	$ 55,043	28.00%	$ 56,584	28.65%	Sell	(1,289.25)	$ 55,295	28.00%
International Bond Fund	$ 13,761	7.00%	$ 14,353	7.27%	Sell	(528.72)	$ 13,824	7.00%
Stocks (65%):	$127,779	65.00%	$126,546	64.08%			$128,364	65.00%
Domestic Large Cap	$ 89,445	45.50%	$ 84,973	43.03%	Buy	4,881.70	$ 89,855	45.50%
Domestic Small Cap	$ 19,167	9.75%	$ 21,371	10.82%	Sell	(2,116.45)	$ 19,255	9.75%
Emerging Market Index Fund	$ 19,167	9.75%	$ 20,202	10.23%	Sell	(947.27)	$ 19,255	9.75%
Total	$196,583	100.00%	$197,483	100.00%			$197,483	100.00%

Chapter 7

Retiring

Making sure you're ready for retirement is a lot like prepping your car for long cross-country drive. Before setting out on the long drive, you'll have your car thoroughly checked over by a qualified mechanic, make sure all routine maintenance is up to date, and you might even do things like buy new tires, get new brakes, or perform other such preventative maintenance. All of this preparation is done so that you can have a smooth uneventful drive across the country.

However, all the preparation of the world can't guarantee you won't be hit by some other driver on your way, be subjected to poor road conditions that give you a flat tire, or experience other such unforeseen problems.

Getting ready for retirement is very similar. You should sit down and take stock of your investments, other sources of income, Social Security, and other assets that are there to provide for a long smooth retirement.

Nonetheless, all you can do is control what's within your control.

Many people are curious about what is the right amount of savings for retirement is. The aggregate retirement income deficit for all Baby Boomers and Gen Xers—the amount by which their savings, plus Social Security falls short of what they need—is $4.3 trillion, according to the Employee Benefit Research Institute. Obviously, people are not saving enough for their retirement years. According to the Plan Sponsor Council of America, the average employee saves only 6.4% of their paycheck in their 401K plan. Most experts say 10% is the minimum to be saved for retirement and for those who are late to start, more like 15%—20%.

Is there some universal formula that will tell me when I've saved enough to guarantee a long smooth retirement? Unfortunately, we don't get the same level of mechanical precision with our retirement plan as we do with our automobile. So you need to prepare for the unexpected with more than you'll need, and spend less than you have in order that you do not outlive your savings.

When it comes to actually figuring out how much to save for a comfortable retirement most employees are on-their-own. Worse, once they retire they have to figure out how to turn their nest egg into a life-long stream of income. Spend too much and you could out live your money. According to a MetLife study, only 28% of employers offer automatic projections of how much retirement income a participant's 401K account might produce.

Rather than providing information unique to an employee, most companies offer generic forecasting tools that make baseline assumptions. The employee's actual investment mix, time horizon to retirement may not be adequately considered. The result could be longevity risk.

Longevity Risk is the risk that you out live your money. The best way to hedge longevity risk is to properly monitor your 401K plan assets and save, save, save. Some advisers will use long-term care insurance as a further risk management tool to protect against outliving your money.

The Journey

One of the first things people will do planning for a cross-country trip is estimate the miles to drive. Then, knowing their mileage per gallon and an estimate for the cost of gas across various states, they can set aside a reasonable budget for gasoline. But the actual course driven can have a material effect on how many miles you drive and how much gasoline you will consume. You may want to take side trips on your cross-country journey. However, these extra miles may not be in your budget and you may have to skip them.

It's very similar with your retirement planning. You'll want to have sufficient income in retirement to allow for various vacations, a comfortable lifestyle, a new car every so often, and enough discretionary income that you can treat yourself to small things here and there.

In order to hit this goal you clearly need to have a sizable nest egg. Many retirement experts will tell you that the most important consideration in the determination of the actual size of your particular retirement nest egg is how much money you make leading up to retirement. I disagree. For me, the most important consideration in the determination of the actual size of your particular retirement nest egg is not how much you *earn* but how much you *spend*.

In the years leading up to retirement most people have satisfied or paid their biggest expenses. Examples of such would be funding children's college tuition and paying off your home mortgage. In addition, most people have their wages peaked in their fifties and then either flat line or drift downward into their sixties. So in the years leading up to retirement your personal cash flow is likely to be very strong, stronger than it's been in your entire working career. Being a well-paid experienced senior employee, coupled with most of your major expenditures being behind you, can put you in a terrific cash flow situation in those final years leading up to retirement.

Now this may not be the case for each and every person but in general it's true. These are great years to substantially top-off your retirement nest egg. But still you say, "When do I know that I have enough?"

In a study published in 1994, Bill Bengen, a financial planner in Southern California, coined the "four percent rule" for retirement withdrawals. In his study he showed that if retirees withdrew four percent of their nest egg in the first year and then increased future withdraws only enough to keep pace with inflation that their nest egg would easily last thirty years.

So if you're retiring at age sixty-five and used the four percent rule, you should expect your nest egg to last approximately thirty years. According to the World Bank the life expectancy for Americans is currently 78.1 years. So depending on your current family history, health and other characteristics, budgeting for a thirty-year retirement through to age ninety-five is not a bad place to start.

Assuming that you want to retire at age sixty-five and have your nest egg last for thirty years, you next need to determine how much money you will need in your first year of retirement. Like our cross-country drive analogy, this is where we have to do some careful planning and mapping to make sure that we get it right.

The first thing I suggest you do to estimate how much you need per year to retire is to take a good careful look through your checkbook, or bank statement, over the past year. If you use any form of money software like Microsoft Money or Quicken, this will be a breeze to do. If not, you just need to take out your checkbook and start journaling expenses.

After a few months you'll see a likely pattern settling into place. You'll see expenses for things like housing, food, gasoline, various utilities (electric, gas, cable television, high-speed Internet, cell phones), insurance, entertainment, gifts, charitable contributions, purchases of various items such as a television, new iPhone, and vacations. With a good handle on your monthly and yearly expenses you can begin to know if you're getting close to being retirement ready.

So let's suppose that you need $50,000 a year to live comfortably in retirement. Using the four percent rule we would divide $50,000 by 0.04 to get your minimum retirement nest egg estimate of $1,250,000.

However much money you need per year to live comfortably right now, just divide it by 0.04. You can use the worksheet below to see how your situation is going.

Retirement Ready Worksheet—Funds Needed to Retire	
Annual living expenses	$
Divide the above by 0.4	
This is how much you will need to retire:	$

Compare this result to your retirement assets and you'll know how close or how far you are from retirement. If you do this exercise and don't like the answer, just like our cross-country driving trip you may have to alter your course. You may have to cut back on some of your retirement spending in order to live within your means. Alternatively, more and more people today are working in retirement as a means to supplement their nest egg or to defer tapping their nest egg until it has sufficiently grown to meet their needs. So if you needed $50,000 a year to live and your nest egg is only $750,000, you can figure out how much money you would need to make to supplement your retirement income. Take the $750,000 retirement nest egg and multiply it by .04 to get $30,000. The $20,000 shortfall would have to be earned through some other form of income or part-time job. By playing around with this very simple yet helpful four percent rule tool you can carry out various retirement scenarios without the need for sophisticated retirement planning software.

So that you can continually adapt your plan and savings patterns, this "retirement ready" exercise should be done well before you actually get close to retirement age. If you do this analysis at age fifty-five and see that you're going to be far off your goal, you can try increasing your savings or pay down debt in order that you might hit your goal and be able to retire comfortably when you choose.

Retirement Ready Worksheet—Additional Savings Needed	
(A) Actual Funds saved:	$
(B) Funds needed for comfortable retirement:	$
(A—B = C) Funding (shortfall)/excess:	$
(D) Years until retirement:	Years
(C divided by D = E) Annual savings needed to achieve goal:	$
(F) Pay Periods per year (ex. 26):	Periods
(E divided F) per pay savings amount:	$ payroll deduction for 401K

Based on the results of your situation you can determine how ready you are for retirement. Compare the result from the above worksheet to your total savings, your contribution plus the employer match, to determine how well you are saving. If you cannot afford to fully fund your per payroll savings requirement, you can adjust your horizon and plan to work longer. Or, as discussed you could assume some level of employment to fill-in and funding needs while in retirement.

Chapter 8

529 Plans

Side benefits

In an earlier chapter I related the personal story about my first experience with the financial adviser's recommendation of a 529 program. I won't relay the story here but suffice it to say that experience triggered my intense interest in understanding how mutual funds work.

I also explained in a previous chapter how I became curious about 401K plans. With a finance background I became increasingly frustrated at my inability to squeeze every possible value dollar out of my plan. I found out that the plans are so complicated and so wrapped in fees that it is quite challenging for even a finance professional to extract maximum value out of the substandard plan.

These two events combined led me to this book. I believe there are so many benefits that you can get by simply understanding how mutual funds work and how institutional programs such as 401Ks, 529s, and IRAs work. By using my system to analyze mutual funds and to understand the mechanics of how these various programs work anyone can take over control of their investment management.

The world-famous CNBC *Mad Money* host, Jim Cramer, often talks in his daily program about how "home gamers" can learn enough about how the stock market works that they can credibly manage their own investments. I do not disagree; however, properly researching an individual stock and its industry requires a huge time commitment that I suspect most viewers simply do not have the time for.

I think many viewers somewhat blindly follow the recommendations of Mr. Cramer without doing substantial independent due diligence of their own. I must admit that I'm guilty of such things myself. Even though I know better, I certainly have bought stock based upon Jim's recommendation on his program. In some cases the recommendations paid out and in many cases they did not. Sometimes I suspect Mr. Cramer just gets a little too enthusiastic about stock. Perhaps he likes the company's CEO or believes he has some deep insight into the prospects of a particular company. As I said, sometimes he does and sometimes he doesn't.

Nonetheless, in his three books on stock picking and investing he lays out a logical program for analyzing individual stocks. If his program is followed with diligence I believe it will lead to more good stock selections than bad ones. The problem is, it takes so much time to analyze an individual stock that many people look for the shortcut and sometimes regret it.

Analyzing mutual funds is not nearly as complicated as analyzing an individual stock. Once you buy into the mutual fund concept the next question really is, which fund should I buy? This book was written to help you quickly and easily answer that question without as much effort as it takes to analyze one company stock. For the most part, mutual funds are safe investments that offer an investor the benefits of professional management, diversification, sector selection, and access to companies whose stock may be unavailable to the general public. Using the approach laid out in this book to analyze 401Ks, you can readily examine and analyze a 529 plan.

Start by getting the prospectus and reading about the program fees, unique benefits for in-state residents, and mutual fund choices offered. There are websites like www.boards.com that summarize key attributes of 529 plans in each state. Use this as your initial screen. Then, look for the fund families the program offers. I happen to be very partial to the Vanguard funds because of their steadfast commitment to low fees. That is part of the reason why I selected the New York 529 plan for my own children. The key is just to understand what it is you're buying and then make an informed decision.

In the section on 401K plans, we talked about the importance of asset allocation, investment horizon, and rebalancing. These three attributes will serve you well with a 529 plan, too. Look at your child's number of years before entering college and how long you plan for them to be in college, and that will determine your investment horizon. Knowing your investment horizon, you can choose an appropriate asset allocation that affords you growth opportunities without the risk of a down market the year before your child goes off to school.

Lastly, once you set your initial asset allocation monitor its performance and do an annual tune-up to ensure your investments, stay on track. It's the same process we follow in our 401K plans and easily translates to a 529. However, the same risks are present, too.

The fund managers in 529 Plans often exhibit the same wide variations in asset mix we saw in Lifestyle funds. The difference between an age-based plan's most and least aggressive holdings can vary widely and be out-of-sync with your personal risk appetite. For example,

It was reported that the direct-sold College Savings Iowa 529 plan, the most aggressive age-based option leaves 20% in stocks when a child is in college. The least aggressive plan had 0% in stocks. Just as we saw with Lifestyle funds, age-based options with the same purported risk level can vary widely between plans. The NY 529 College Savings Program Direct Plan's moderate-risk option has no money invested in stocks at the point right before your child enters college. Whereas, the Rhode Island CollegeBound fund's moderate option has 11%—28% in stocks at the same time!

In the end the best thing you can do to prepare for retirement or your children's education is become informed and educated!

Chapter 9

403B Plans

Just like the 401K plan, the 403B name comes from the section of the Internal Revenue Code that made these plans possible. A 403B plan is a U.S. tax-advantaged retirement savings plan available for public education organizations, some non-profit employers (only Internal Revenue Code 501(c)(3) organizations), cooperative hospital service organizations, and self-employed ministers in the United States. It has tax treatment similar to a 401K plan.

In general, many of the rules and contribution limits are the same for both 401K and 403B plans. Contribution rules and catch-up limits are the same for both plans. Annual contribution amounts are as well. Matching policies can vary but in general employer matching in a 403B is the same as employer matching in a 401K plan.

The big difference between 403Bs and 401Ks are the types of investments commonly offered. Many 403B plans only offer annuities sold by insurance companies (see section on variable annuities earlier in the book). With variable annuities, your investment choices can include traditional mutual funds or separate counts, which are like mutual funds but are managed by an insurance company. Variable annuity accounts don't guarantee any return, nor do they guarantee your principal. If you're variable annuity offers mutual funds I suggest you select from those and use the strategies for efficient mutual fund selection and annual portfolio rebalancing that we discuss in this book.

Chapter 10

IRAs

Individual retirement arrangements were introduced in 1974 with the enactment of the Employee Retirement Income Security Act (ERISA). Taxpayers could contribute up to $1,500 a year and reduce their taxable income by the amount of their contributions. Initially, ERISA restricted IRAs to workers who were not covered by a qualified employment-based retirement plan. In 1981, the Economic Recovery Tax Act (ERTA) allowed all taxpayers under the age of 70½ to contribute to an IRA, regardless of their coverage under a qualified plan. It also raised the maximum annual contribution to $2,000 and allowed participants to contribute $250 on behalf of a nonworking spouse. The Tax Reform Act of 1986 phased out the deduction for IRA contributions among higher-earning workers who are covered by an employment-based retirement plan. However, those earning above the amount that allowed deductible contributions could still make nondeductible contributions to their IRA. According to the IRS, "The maximum amount allowed as an IRA contribution was $1500 from 1975 to 1981, $2000 from 1982 to 2001, $3000 from 2002 to 2004, $4000 from 2004 to 2007, and $5000 from 2008 to 2010." Beginning in 2002, those over 50 could make an additional contribution called a "Catch-up Contribution."

IRS Current limitations:

1. An IRA can only be funded with cash or cash equivalents. Attempting to transfer any other type of asset into the IRA is a prohibited transaction and disqualifies the fund from its beneficial tax treatment.
2. Rollovers, transfers, and conversions between IRAs and other retirement arrangements can include any asset.

3. The maximum for an IRA contribution in years 2006 and 2007 was $4,000 for an individual under the age of 50. Individuals aged 50 and older could contribute up to $5,000. For 2008 through 2011, the limit was $5,000 for those under age 50, and $6,000 for those over 50. All contributions must be from income.
4. This limit applied to the sum of contributions to Roth IRAs and traditional IRAs.

For example, a person aged 45 who put $3,500 into a traditional IRA this year so far, can either put $1,500 more into this traditional IRA or $1,500 in a Roth IRA. There may be an additional administrative step needed so that the trustee that holds the IRA proceeds actually re-titles or transfers the $3,500 Traditional proceeds into the Roth category for their internal bookkeeping to survive an IRS audit.

The amount of the IRA contributions (both Traditional and Roth) that can be deducted from current-year taxes is partially reduced for levels of income beyond a threshold, and eliminated entirely beyond another threshold, if the contributor and/or the contributor's spouse is covered by an employer-based retirement plan. The dollar amounts of the thresholds vary depending on tax filing status (single, married, etc.) and on which spouse is covered at work.

There are several types of IRA:

Traditional IRA—contributions are often tax-deductible (often simplified as "money is deposited before tax" or "contributions are made with pre-tax assets"), all transactions and earnings within the IRA have no tax impact, and withdrawals at retirement are taxed as income (except for those portions of the withdrawal corresponding to contributions that were not deducted). Depending upon the nature of the contribution, a traditional IRA may be referred to as a "deductible IRA" or a "non-deductible IRA." It was introduced with the Tax Reform Act (TRA) of 1986.

Roth IRA—contributions are made with after-tax assets, all transactions within the IRA have no tax impact, and withdrawals are usually tax-free. Named for Senator William Roth, Jr. The Roth IRA was introduced as part of the Taxpayer Relief Act of 1997.

SEP IRA—a provision that allows an employer (typically a small business or self-employed individual) to make retirement plan contributions into a Traditional IRA established in the employee's name, instead of to a pension fund in the company's name.

SIMPLE IRA—Savings Incentive Match Plan for Employees that requires employer matching contributions to the plan whenever an employee makes a contribution. The plan is similar to a 401K plan, but with lower contribution limits and simpler (and thus less costly) administration. Although it is termed an IRA, it is treated separately.

Self-directed IRA—a self-directed IRA that permits the account holder to make investments on behalf of the retirement plan.

401K rollovers into IRAs occur many times when an employee leaves their current employer and had 401K plan assets at that employer. The benefit of rolling over the plan assets is that you can gain more control over the funds in the plan. You can expand the investment options when you move the plan assets out of the original 401K plan and into an IRA.

You do not have to move the assets and can leave them in the existing 401K plan. Another option is to transfer the plan assets from the old employer's plan into the plan at your new employer, assuming that the new employer offers a 401K. Personally, I like to have all of my funds together in one plan. My recommendation is that you concentrate your plan assets into one at the current employer.

Glossary

This Glossary is largely comprised of Investment-Related Terms for Disclosures to Retirement Plan Participants. It was developed by The SPARK Institute and the Investment Company Institute. Our use of the definitions developed by them is used with their permission and my gratitude.

12b-1 Fees: Fees paid by a mutual fund out of fund assets to cover the costs of marketing and selling fund shares.

401K Plan: A retirement plan that enables employees to set aside a portion of their compensation in a special account, often with matching contributions from the employer. Contributions and earnings grow tax-deferred until withdrawn—ideally at retirement.

401K Contributions: Voluntary employee contributions that, unlike before-tax elective contributions, are currently included in gross income for current income tax purposes. If a 401K plan is going to provide for designated Roth contributions, it must also offer before-tax elective contributions. Qualified Roth 401K Distributions: The tax rules for distributions from Roth 401K accounts differ significantly from those for traditional 401K accounts. If a distribution is a qualified Roth distribution, the entire distribution, including any earnings, is free from federal tax. Qualified Roth 401K distributions must satisfy two rules (both, not either/or): the five-year rule and the purpose rule. The five-year rule is satisfied if the distribution from the Roth account is made at the end of the 5-year-taxable period following the participant's first Roth contribution. For purposes of the five-year rule, the participant's first Roth contribution is considered contributed on January 1, even if made on December 31, of that same calendar year. If the participant changes employers, a new 5-year period starts with the date of the first Roth 401K contribution to the new employer's plan. However, if the Roth account from the previous employer's plan is rolled over in a direct rollover to the new employer's plan, the previous 5-year-taxable period is kept.

The purpose rule is satisfied if the distribution from the Roth account is attributable to the participant's attainment of age 59 ½, disability, or death. Rate of Return: This represents the return on your investment, including interest, dividends and any other income or growth in the value of your investments.

403B Plan: A U.S. tax-advantaged retirement savings plan available for public education organizations, some non-profit employers (only Internal Revenue Code 501(c)(3) organizations), cooperative hospital service organizations, and self-employed ministers in the United States. It has tax treatment similar to a 401K plan.

529 Savings Plan: State-sponsored program designed to help parents and others finance a child's college expenses. Subject to contribution limitations and investment guidelines. Anyone can contribute, regardless of income level, and the money is generally invested in a portfolio of stocks, bonds or mutual funds. Withdrawals are federal income tax free if used for qualified higher education expenses; withdrawals for non-educational purposes will trigger federal income taxes and a 10 percent tax penalty.

Age Rule: Rule regarding eligibility to contribute to a Traditional IRA. An individual must be under age 70½ for the entire year to make a regular contribution to an IRA.

Annuity (Fixed): Contract under which a series of payments are promised in exchange for a single payment or series of payments.

Asset Allocation: The diversification of investments among several asset classes, such as stocks, bonds, and short-term investments (e.g., cash equivalents). Proper asset allocation may limit risk and increase opportunities.

Asset Class: A category of investments, such as stocks, bonds, or cash equivalents

Back-end Load: A sales charge investors pay when they redeem (or sell) mutual fund shares, insurance products, or other investments, generally used to compensate brokers. Also known as a deferred sales charge.

Balanced Fund: A mutual fund that invests in a combination of asset classes (usually stocks and bonds and, in some cases, cash equivalents). Balanced funds seek to provide growth and income.

Benchmark: A standard against which an investment's performance can be compared, often an index of securities in the same asset class as the investment.

Beneficiary: An individual, institution, trustee or estate which receives, or may become eligible to receive, benefits under a will, insurance policy, retirement plan, annuity or other contract.

Bond: The most common debt security. A bond is basically an "IOU" certifying that the bondholder has loaned money to a corporation or government and describing the terms of the loan payment period and interest rate. A bond usually matures in 10 to 30 years and pays interest at regular intervals. The principal amount of the bond is repaid at maturity. Municipal bonds are bonds issued by a state, local (city) government, or agency.

Certified Financial Planner (CFP): This is a financial planner who has received a license from the Institute of Certified Financial Planners indicating that he/she was trained in investments, budgeting, taxes, banking, estate planning and insurance. Some CFPs work on commission for the products they sell, and some work for a flat hourly fee.

Chartered Financial Analyst (CFA): A designation for investment professional conferred by the CFA Institute formerly known as the Association for Investment Management and Research (AIMR). Candidates are required to meet competency standards and pass multiple exams in quantitative analysis, economics, securities analysis, portfolio management, and financial accounting. Candidates are required to have three years of investment-management experience.

Closed-end Fund: A type of investment company that does not continuously offer new shares for sale but instead sells a fixed number of shares at one time in the initial public offering (IPO). After a fund's IPO, its shares typically trade on a secondary market, such as the New York Stock Exchange. Legally known as a "closed-end company."

Company Matching Contributions: An amount or percent of pay the company will contribute to the employee's retirement plan account typically based on the employee's rate of contribution to the plan. Generally, although the type and amount of company contributions vary, a company may match $0.50 for every $1.00 the employee contributes, up to a maximum percentage of pay, hence the term company match or company matching contribution. The type and amount of a company matching contributions vary and are set by the employer.

Common Stock: Securities that represent an ownership interest and give the investor voting rights in the issuing corporation.

Contingent Deferred Sales Load (Charge): A sales charge that investors pay when they redeem (or sell) mutual fund shares. The amount of the charge depends on the length of time shares were held. After a specified holding period, the charge reaches zero.

Coverdell Education Savings Account (ESA): Investment vehicle designed to help parents or others fund a child's education. Contributions aren't tax deductible, but distributions for qualified educational expenses aren't taxable. Generally, funds in ESAs are transferable among family members. Several restrictions: Entire account must be disbursed by the beneficiary's 30th birthday; withdrawals after this date or for expenses that are not qualified education expenses are subject to federal income taxes and a tax penalty.

Deferred Annuity: Allows for the accumulation of money over time on a tax-deferred basis, with a choice of payout options.

Deferred Sales Charge: A sales charge that investors pay when they redeem (or sell) mutual fund shares, generally used by the fund to compensate brokers. Also known as a back-end load.

Defined Benefit Plan: A qualified plan designed to pay a benefit, typically based on a percentage of salary, at retirement. The employer, not the employee, funds the plan.

Defined Contribution Plan: A qualified retirement plan, such as a 401K plan, whose benefits depend on the amount contributed by the employee/ employer and the earnings of those contributions.

Direct Rollover: The movement of funds from a qualified retirement plan into an IRA without the account owner taking receipt of the funds.

Distribution: Withdrawing funds from a retirement savings plan.

Diversification: Portfolio strategy designed to reduce exposure to risk by combining a variety of investments unlikely to have the same volatility, such as stocks, bonds and real estate. Not all asset classes or industries or individual companies move up and down in value at the same time or at the same rate, which may limit volatility. Diversification helps reduce the upside and downside potential and allows for more consistent performance under a wide range of economic conditions, but does not assure a profit or protect against loss in a declining market.

Dividend: In a mutual fund, a distribution of investment income earned by the fund.

Early (premature) Withdrawal: A withdrawal of funds from an IRA, a 401K plan, or any tax qualified retirement plan, usually before age 59½. Early withdrawals are subject to tax penalties, though there are some exceptions.

Employer-sponsored Retirement Plan: A Defined Contribution or Defined Benefit retirement plan. The most common types are 401K, Profit Sharing Plans and Pension Plans. Other types include SEP, Keogh and SIMPLE plans.

Excess Contribution: Any IRA contribution that exceeds the maximum contribution limits permitted by law. Penalty taxes apply for each year an excess contribution exists.

Exchange-traded Fund (ETF): A type of investment company whose shares trade on stock exchanges at prices determined by the market. Compare to mutual fund.

Expense Ratio: On a mutual fund, the operating expenses, including investment management, administrative and other costs, expressed as a percentage of the assets.

Fixed-income Securities: Investments with specified payment dates and amounts, primarily bonds that pay interest.

Front-End Load: A sales charge applied initially to each deposit. The starting value of the investment is the amount deposited less the sales charge applied.

Global Fund: A fund that invests in stocks throughout the world, including the United States. See International Fund to understand the difference.

Growth Fund: A mutual fund whose manager buys primarily high-growth stocks for the fund's portfolio with the expectation that these stocks will increase in value. The stock of a growth firm is one whose earnings are generally growing faster than the economy or market norm. Investment risk with growth stock tends to be high. Generally speaking these stock have high P/E multiples, do not pay dividends and are younger firms.

Individual Retirement Account (IRA): An individual retirement account, or IRA, is a personal savings plan trusteed by a bank or a qualified nonbank trustee. It allows you to set aside money for retirement, while offering you tax advantages. IRAs cannot be owned jointly. However, any amounts remaining in your IRA upon your death can be paid to your beneficiary or beneficiaries. Types of IRAs include the Traditional IRA, Simple IRA, Education IRA or Coverdell Education Savings Account, and the Roth IRA.

IRA Rollover: The movement of IRA funds from one IRA provider or qualified retirement plan to the account owner, and then to another IRA provider. The account owner has 60 days to complete this transaction before the transaction is considered a taxable distribution of funds.

IRA Transfer: The movement of IRA funds directly from one IRA provider to another without the IRA owner taking receipt of the funds. This transaction is sometimes referred to as a Trustee to Trustee transfer.

Immediate Annuity: Allows for the conversion of a sum of money into a guaranteed series of payments for a period equal to the greater of a person's life or a specified number of years.

Individual Retirement Account (IRA): Tax-deferred retirement account for an individual that permits individuals to set aside up to $5,000 per year (for tax year 2012 and an additional $1,000 for those 50 or older), with earnings tax-deferred until withdrawals begin at age 59½ or later (or earlier, with a 10% tax penalty). Only those who do not participate in a pension plan at work or who do participate and meet certain income guidelines can make deductible contributions to a Traditional IRA. Such contributions are deductible from income in that year and any growth accumulates tax-deferred until the funds are withdrawn. All others can make contributions to a Traditional IRA on a non-deductible basis.

Interest: The price paid by borrowers for the use of money. Companies, governments and municipalities (borrowers) pay interest to investors (lenders) who purchase their bonds.

International Fund: A fund that invests in stocks of companies outside the United States. See Global Fund to understand the difference.

Investment Adviser: Generally, a person or entity that receives compensation for giving individually tailored advice on investing in stocks, bonds, or mutual funds. Some investment advisers also manage portfolios of securities, including mutual funds.

Investment Management and Administrative Charge: Expenses for managing and administering the assets in the separate accounts offered under the group annuity contract.

Large-cap Fund: A fund that invests in the stocks of "large" companies (as measured by market capitalization or the value of a company's outstanding stock).

Lifecycle Fund: A diversified mutual fund that automatically shifts towards a more conservative mix of investments as it approaches a particular year in the future, known as its "target date." A lifecycle fund investor picks a fund with the right target date based on his or her particular investment goal.

Long-term Care Insurance: Provides coverage for necessary medical or personal care services outside of a hospital setting, such as in a nursing home or the insured's home.

Management Fee: A fee paid out of fund assets to the fund's investment adviser or its affiliates for managing the fund's portfolio, any other management fees payable to the fund's investment adviser or its affiliates, and any administrative fees payable to the investment adviser that are not included in the "other expenses" category.

Market Index: A measurement of the performance of a specific "basket" of stocks, bonds, or other type of investment considered to represent a particular market or sector of the stock or bond markets, or the economy.

Market Risk: The chance that the value of investments will not grow as expected or may even decline in value.

Matching Contributions: An employer contribution to an individual's 401K account based on the amount the individual contributes. For example, the employer may match 50 cents for every dollar the individual contributes.

Medicaid: Program funded by the federal and state governments that pays for medical care for those unable to afford it.

Medicare: Federal Health Insurance for the Aged program, provided under the Social Security Act.

Mid-cap Fund: Invests in the stocks of "mid-size" companies (as measured by market capitalization or the market value of a company's outstanding stock).

Money Market Account: Savings account insured by the federal government that offers many of the same services as checking accounts although transactions are somewhat more limited. Can be convenient for storing money to be used for upcoming investments or received from the sale of recent investments. Although very safe and highly liquid, may offer a lower interest rate than other investments.

Money Market Instruments: Forms of debt that mature in less than one year. These investments are easily converted to cash. U.S. Treasury bills make up the bulk of trading in the money markets.

Mutual Fund: A professionally managed pool of stocks, bonds and other securities, which are owned "mutually" by the fund's investors in proportion to their investment in the fund. The amount of risk varies among the different investments in the fund. In this way, your investment is diversified.

Net Asset Value (NAV): The price or market value of an individual share of a security or mutual fund. In the case of a mutual fund, the net asset value is calculated daily and is determined by adding up the value of all the securities and cash in a fund's portfolio, subtracting liabilities if there are any, and dividing that number by the number of shares the fund has issued. Except for money market funds, which generally strive to maintain a NAV of $1.00 per share, the share value will usually change daily.

Operating Expenses: The costs a fund incurs in connection with running the fund, including management fees, distribution (12b-1) fees, and other expenses. Operating expenses are paid from a fund's assets before earnings are distributed to shareholders.

Pension: Post-retirement benefits an employee receives from an employer?s retirement plan.

Portfolio: A collection of investment holdings either in a fund or in one's personal account.

Preferred Stock: Class of stock that pays dividends at a specified rate and that has preference over common stock in the payment of dividends and/ or upon liquidation of company assets.

Pre-Tax Contributions: An amount or percentage of pay an employee elects to direct from pay, before taxes are calculated and withheld, and contribute to his or her retirement plan account.

Principal: Amount borrowed, or part of the amount borrowed, which remains unpaid, excluding interest. Also considered the original amount invested or deposited.

Qualified Retirement Plan: Is a retirement plan approved by the IRS that allows for tax-deferred contributions and accumulation of investment income. Individual Retirement Accounts (IRA) and 401K plans are examples of qualified retirement plans.

Qualified Roth 401K Account: Is a separate account under a 401K plan to which designated Roth contributions are made, and for which separate accounting of contributions, gains, and losses is maintained. Qualified Roth

Rebalancing: Bringing a portfolio back to its original (or a desired) asset allocation mix.

Redemption Fee: A shareholder fee that some mutual funds charge when investors redeem (or sell) mutual fund shares. The fee is typically applicable to redemptions made soon after purchase.

Registered Investment Adviser (RIA): Registered investment advisors are licensed and supervised by the SEC and the appropriate state securities board. Registry with the SEC requires the submission of an application and associated processing fees. Some states require investment advisors to pass the Series 65 Uniform Term Investment Advisers Exam before they are granted a practicing license. Registered investment advisors are subject to random audits after registry.

Required Beginning Date (RBD): The deadline by which an IRA owner must take his or her first Required Minimum Distribution. The RBD is April 1 after the year in which the IRA owner turns age 70½.

Required Minimum Distribution (RMD): The minimum dollar amount an IRA owner must withdraw each year beginning when he or she reaches age 70½, as required by the IRS.

Retirement Age: Typically, most pension plans set age 65 as the normal retirement age. However, for Social Security purposes, your normal retirement age, the age at which you can collect unreduced Social Security retirement benefits ranges from 65 to 67, based on your date of birth.

Return: The profit (or loss) earned (incurred) through investing.

Risk Tolerance: An investor's ability or willingness to endure declines in the value of investments in exchange for a greater potential investment return.

Rollover: Tax-free movement of funds from a qualified retirement plan into an IRA or other qualified plan within a specific time frame (60 days). Or, a movement of funds from one tax qualified account to another.

Rollover IRA: An IRA established to hold the assets of an eligible distribution from a qualified plan.

Roth 401K: The Roth 401K feature permits eligible plan participants, regardless of their income, to make after tax contributions to a qualified Roth account. In addition, qualified distributions from a Roth 401K account are free from federal tax.

Roth IRA: A Roth IRA differs from traditional IRA's in that contributions are not deductible and can be made only by taxpayers that fall below certain AGI (adjusted gross income) levels. Unlike a traditional IRA, contributions may be made after age 70½. Distributions made after the 5-year-taxable period, beginning with the first year a contribution was made to a Roth IRA set up for your benefit, are not taxable if made either:

1. After you are 59 ½
2. Because you are disabled
3. To a beneficiary or your estate after your death
4. To buy, build or rebuild a first home

S&P 500 Stock: A composite index of 500 large company stocks compiled by Standard & Poor's Corporation that is used as a broad measure of U.S. stock market performance.

Self-directed IRA: An IRA that allows the individual to select the investment options that best fit their investment objectives. The investment choices include stocks, bonds, mutual funds and other funds and other investment vehicles, Certificate of Deposits and other savings vehicles.

Simplified Employee Pension Plan (SEP): An employer-sponsored retirement plan that is designed for owners of small businesses or self-employed individuals. Contributions are tax-deductible and earnings tax-deferred. Qualified individuals can contribute a fixed percentage of their earned net income (up to $49,000 maximum for 2011). SEPs are more flexible, easier to set up, and simpler to administer than many other qualified plans.

Small-cap Fund: Invests in the stocks of relatively "small" publicly traded companies (as measured by market capitalization or the total market value of a company's outstanding stock).

Social Security: Disability and retirement program established under the federal Social Security Act of the Railroad Retirement Act.

Surrender Charge: A sales charge incurred when an investor withdraws money from an annuity within a certain period after purchase.

Standard of Living: A broad measurement of a person's way of life, covering factors such as pay, geographic area, home, vehicle ownership and the ability to afford luxuries like vacations. A goal in financial planning is to maintain the same, if not better, standard of living in retirement as during your working career.

Stock: The capital invested in a company or corporation through the buying of shares, each of which entitles the buyer to a part of the ownership. When individuals or institutions buy the stocks, they become owners of a piece of the corporation. This ownership interest is called "equity."

Target Date Fund: A diversified mutual fund that automatically shifts towards a more conservative mix of investments as it approaches a particular year in the future, known as its "target date." A target fund investor picks a fund with the right target date based on his or her particular investment goal.

Traditional IRA: A traditional IRA is what most people think of when they think of an IRA. The IRS uses the term "traditional" to distinguish it from any other form of IRA. Any individual with compensation for a calendar year may contribute to a traditional IRA, however you must be under age 70 ½ at the end of the calendar year. Whether a contribution to a traditional IRA is deductible will depend on the individual's gross income and whether the individual is an active participant in a qualified plan. A single traditional IRA can accept both deductible and non-deductible contributions. Withdrawals taken before age 59 ½ may be subject to a 10% tax penalty.

Treasury Bills: Short-term U.S. government debt securities that have maturities of one year or less that is sold at weekly auctions at a discount and is redeemed at face value.

Treasury Bonds: Long-term U.S. government debt securities that have maturities of more than ten years.

Treasury Notes: Intermediate-term U.S. government debt securities that have maturities between one and ten years.

Uniform Gifts/Transfers to Minors Act: Law enacted in most states that permits an adult (the custodian) to own property for the exclusive benefit of a minor. At the direction of the custodian, control over money in an UGMA/UTMA account is transferred automatically to the beneficiary when he or she reaches the age specified in the state's UGMA/UTMA statute.

Unit Value: The value of each unit in an investment account class within a separate account. This value is determined daily by dividing the ending market value of the separate account allocable to that class reduced by the applicable Investment Management Charge and Administrative Charge, by the total number of units in that class prior to any deposits or withdrawals on that day. The total number of units in that class is then increased for deposits and decreased for withdrawals at the unit value for that day.

Value Fund: A mutual fund whose manager buys primarily undervalued stocks for the fund's portfolio with the expectation that these stocks will increase in value. Generally speaking, value stocks are more mature and have lower P/E multiples, have slow or declining revenue and have high dividends yields.

Variable Annuity: Life insurance annuity contract that provides future payments to the holder, usually at retirement. Payment size depends on the performance of the portfolio's securities.

Vested: For a retirement savings plan participant, vesting refers to the gradual granting of ownership of contributions made by your employer.

Will: Legally enforceable declaration directing the disposal of a deceased person?s probate property.

Yield: The annual dividend or interest payment an investor expects to receive, divided by the price of the stock or bond.